ROUTLEDGE LIBRARY EDITIONS:
ECONOMICS AND SOCIETY

Volume 22

# PLANNING AND ECONOMIC GROWTH

# PLANNING AND ECONOMIC GROWTH

A. K. DAS-GUPTA

Routledge
Taylor & Francis Group
LONDON AND NEW YORK

First published in 1965 by George Allen & Unwin Ltd.

This edition first published in 2026
by Routledge
4 Park Square, Milton Park, Abingdon, Oxon OX14 4RN

and by Routledge
605 Third Avenue, New York, NY 10158

*Routledge is an imprint of the Taylor & Francis Group, an informa business*



*British Library Cataloguing in Publication Data*
A catalogue record for this book is available from the British Library

ISBN: 978-1-032-97576-4 (Set)
ISBN: 978-1-041-12992-9 (Volume 22) (hbk)
ISBN: 978-1-041-12995-0 (Volume 22) (pbk)
ISBN: 978-1-003-66756-8 (Volume 22) (ebk)

DOI: 10.4324/9781003667568

**Publisher's Note**
The publisher has gone to great lengths to ensure the quality of this reprint but points out that some imperfections in the original copies may be apparent.

**Disclaimer**
The publisher has made every effort to trace copyright holders and would welcome correspondence from those they have been unable to trace.

# PLANNING AND ECONOMIC GROWTH

*by*

A. K. DAS-GUPTA

*Professor of International Finance,*
*Indian School of International Studies;*
*Formerly Professor of Economics, Banaras Hindu University*

*London*

GEORGE ALLEN & UNWIN LTD

RUSKIN HOUSE, MUSEUM STREET

FIRST PUBLISHED IN 1965



PRINTED IN GREAT BRITAIN
*in 10 point Times Roman type*
BY C. TINLING AND CO. LTD.,
LIVERPOOL, LONDON AND PRESCOT

*To*

*Bibi and Partha*

# PREFACE

This is a collection of papers which I wrote over the last decade or so. They relate by and large to problems of economic development and have special reference to the Indian experience in planning. Thus, although the papers were written at different times and under different sets of circumstances, there is a certain common base to which in general they are linked; most of the topics dealt with arose out of my reflections on planning and economic growth. Hence the title.

The volume is divided into four parts. Part I starts with a general survey of the development of economic theory, showing in particular the contrast between the marginalist theory of allocation of resources and the modern theory of growth. The chief emphasis here is on the need for an analysis of the interrelation between the over-all growth of an economy and the movement of relative prices. Where, it is argued, an accelerated rate of growth is imposed upon an economy through planning, there the allocation of resources has to be disentangled from normal market forces and the movement of relative prices, in so far as these latter are inconsistent with the required rate of accumulation. The alternative, it may be mentioned here, is control of individual incomes, so as to maintain via demand a system of relative prices which would conform to the required allocation of resources.

The remaining papers, with the exception of 'Thoughts on Finance', are devoted to an analysis of unemployment in an over-populated, under-developed economy, such as India, and of the relation of investment to employment. Particular reference is made to the size of investment in India's Third Five Year Plan, and a criterion in terms of employment is suggested for choosing the target for investment. The minimum of investment called for, it is contended, is one which would ensure an increase of employment over time in proportion to the increase in labour force consequent on the growth of population, without a deterioration in the productivity of labour. This, let it be remembered, is a more modest criterion than was chosen by the Planning Commission for the Second Plan; indeed it is a precarious minimum, considering that the initial backlog of unemployed in the economy was itself not inconsiderable. Yet experience does not hold out any better prospect for the Plan.

'Thoughts on Finance' was intended as a seminar paper for consideration in connection with India's extraordinary defence finance necessitated by the Chinese aggression of October, 1962.

The paper is included here because some of the ideas that it contains have relevance to development finance, too.

The title of Part II is derived from the paper on 'Economic Development and Relative Prices', where an attempt is made in terms of inter-sectoral expenditure flows to analyse the effect of planned economic development on relative prices. The analysis suggests, as I noticed earlier, the need for control of prices in a planned economy. The paper on 'The Theory of Black Market Prices', although originally written with reference to the inflation and price control of the late forties, has thus application to similar problems arising out of planned economic development. The earlier paper ('The Use of Curves in the Analysis of Market Price') deals with the problem of price formation under 'stationary conditions' and would, I am afraid, appear to be out of place in this collection. It is included here because of its importance, as I would judge it, as a base for an understanding of the transition from statics to dynamics.[1]

The papers that form Part III deal with certain international aspects of economic growth. The central question asked is whether, in a developing economy, foreign exchange does or does not pose a problem which is distinct from the problem of domestic saving—whether, that is, the 'balance of payments barrier', to quote Dr I. G. Patel,[2] lies in such an economy *inside* or *outside* the 'inflation barrier'. I have often noticed in discussions a certain strange affinity on this question between staunch free-traders on the one hand and socialist planners on the other—both arguing that the real bottle-neck in a developing economy is one of domestic saving and that the problem of foreign exchange, if anything, is subsidiary to it. My own attitude on the question, as will be evident from a comparison of 'Foreign Balance in a Developing Economy' with the earlier paper on 'The Relation of Foreign Aid to Domestic Investment', has mellowed over the years largely as a result of the persuasion of Dr Ashok Mitra; but it has not been altogether modified.

A word of explanation is perhaps needed for the inclusion under Part IV of a bunch of papers that deal not with economics as such but with the teaching of economics and allied problems. They would appear to be out of tune with the rest of the book both in regard to subject matter and in regard to approach; they are indeed more of the nature of 'views'. My excuse for including them in this collection is that the problems with which they deal have their origin in India's planning and economic development. Planning of education is surely an important part of the general planning of an economy, and

[1] Special attention is drawn to this transition in Sec. 2 of 'Tendencies in Economic Theory', below.

[2] See I. G. Patel, 'Trade and Payment Policy', *International Trade Theory in a Developing Economy* (London, 1963), edited by Roy Harrod, p. 310.

any misdirection and unbalance in the former is destined to vitiate the latter. The concern shown in some of these papers is just an acknowledgment of this possibility.

I belong to a generation of economists who would attach much greater importance to price analysis than to the analysis of economic growth. In our undergraduate days in the university, we would be asked to concentrate on Book V of Marshall's *Principles*; Book IV would be referred to only in passing. As I recollect now, the procedure was not altogether satisfying to me in those youthful days. 'How is a mere adjustment in the distribution of resources, however perfect it may be,' I remember I would often ask myself in those days, 'to solve the problem of poverty with which Marshall opens his enquiry into the principles of economics?' Apparently I was not brave enough to pursue the query. And as later I got involved at the London School of Economics in the mid-thirties in indifference curves and isoquants, the query itself lost its sharpness.

Like so many others, I crossed the neo-classical boundary through Keynes's *General Theory*, although unlike so many others, less as a convert than as a critic, so far as its application to Indian conditions was concerned. I would not deny the possible existence of some involuntary unemployment in India. After all India is a vast country with wide enough variety of economic contours to provide accommodation for both Keynes and, say, Marx. However, insufficiency of effective demand and involuntary unemployment, I would argue, could be dismissed as of minor consequence, while the central problem of the Indian economy—mass unemployment and poverty—was to be explained in terms of insufficient accumulation of capital. Thus the solution of the problem of unemployment in India, I would say, lay not in movements along a *given* demand curve for labour—for such movements would be severely restricted in view of the minimum subsistence barrier, but in *shifts* in the demand curve made possible by additions to the stock of capital. It is this proposition that I developed in a course of extension lectures on 'Full Employment for India' that I gave to the University of Lucknow in the autumn of 1949, a summary of which appears in this volume under the title 'Keynesian Economics and Under-developed Countries'. From this to an acceptance of planning as the instrument for the mobilization of resources for economic development, such as India officially adopted within a couple of years, was but a natural step.

My education in planning and growth economics has been helped considerably by discussions with friends. I should mention two among them in particular, Dr S. R. Sen and Professor A. K. Sen, with whom I spent many profitable evenings over the last few years.

## *Preface*

The papers collected here were previously published in various journals. While revising them, I felt it necessary to make certain verbal alterations here and there and to eliminate certain topical references which have since lost their interest. I should thank the editors of the journals in which the papers were originally published for their courtesy in permitting me to reprint them. My special thanks are due to the editor of *The Economic Weekly*, Mr Sachin Chaudhuri, without whose promptings most of these papers would not have been written.

Finally, I must express my appreciation of the honour that the Association of Commonwealth Universities, London, and the Faculty of Economics, University of Cambridge, showed me by inviting me to a Visiting Fellowship which brought me here early this session. It is the quiet that I have had the privilege of enjoying at Cambridge that gave me the impulse to collect these papers and to edit them for publication.

Cambridge
June, 1964

A. K. DAS-GUPTA.

## CONTENTS

*Contents*

PART IV: TEACHING ECONOMICS

# *Part I*

# GROWTH AND EMPLOYMENT

# 1

# TENDENCIES IN ECONOMIC THEORY*

## I

Economic theory—in the form in which we have it today—is just about two hundred years old. Considering its age, it has made remarkable progress. We have travelled far since the days of the pioneers. There is hardly any field of economic theory which has escaped some kind of reformulation or retouching at some stage in its career over the last century and a half. Yet who among us would have the temerity to suggest, despite all the developments that have taken place in this or that field, that we have succeeded as yet to hit upon a determinate goal which economic theory is expected to lead up to? We have travelled far, but we have not always travelled along routes that are convergent. We have had 'epochs' of economic theory—Classical, Marginalist and Modern—each having a distinct terrain, and not quite assimilated into the other.

There is indeed a certain lack of continuity in the development of economic theory. The reason for this is perhaps partly political. Partly also it must lie in the very nature of our science. The function of economic theory is to raise questions concerning economic phenomena as they emerge in society from time to time, and to indicate the mode of answering them. The character of economic theory is thus moulded by the type of questions that assume importance in a given environmental setting—though it is of the nature of 'theory' that once it is derived, it takes a form which makes it transcend the particular setting that gives it birth.

Why do prices rise? How do trade restrictions affect the prices of goods and the economy as a whole? What is the significance of a market for the development of an economy? How do movements of prices affect the earnings of different classes of a society—and how does distribution of wealth in its turn affect economic growth? What sort of relation exists between the growth of wealth and the growth of numbers? These are some of the questions that cropped up in England in the late eighteenth century and early nineteenth, as she was passing through a stage of what is known as Industrial Revolution. Attempts at answering questions such as these with reference to

* Presidential Address to the *43rd Annual Conference of the Indian Economic Association*, omitting Sec. IV. Originally published in *The Indian Economic Journal*, Vol. VIII, No. 3, January, 1961.

the particular setting in which they arose gave birth to Classical Political Economy. Man's struggle against nature and his triumph in securing higher standards of living, impediments to progress created by injudicious regulatory laws, the dampening effect of population growth, the possible conflict in social relations that the process of growth tends to generate—these constitute the background against which the classical system developed, and it is against this background that classical theories have to be seen if they are to be judged properly.

Here was a small island, already commercially developed, which was in the midst of large scale technological innovations, supported by a spirit of enterprise never before experienced elsewhere, where population was growing fast and pressing on the 'means of subsistence', where the unbalance thus created between the price of agriculture and the price of manufacture was further accentuated by restrictions on the import of corn and other mercantilist devices. The problem was to show the way how the spirit of enterprise that was released in the wake of the industrial revolution might have full play, and adequate resources might be mobilized to give effect to all the technical progress that had been taking place in the field of manufactures. In this perspective the characteristic classical theories would all appear to fall into their places. Combine Smith's theory of division of labour with the Ricardian theory of rent and the Malthusian theory of population, and you have via the labour theory of value an explanation of the movement of 'corn' prices *vis-à-vis* manufactures. Follow it up with the classical theory of surplus, conceived either in terms of Smith's 'productive labour' or in terms of Ricardo's 'net revenue', and you have the role of capital as the determinant of economic progress. The theory of foreign trade comes in as part of the system in so far as an extension of the market, like innovations, tends to keep up the volume of investible surplus and hence of capital.

The initial impulse to progress comes from saving. Where enterprise exists, the saving that generates in the economy is turned towards the formation of capital. Income increases and with it the investible surplus. There is, however, the retarding effect of growth of numbers, the degree of retardation depending upon the relative rates of capital accumulation and population growth. If accumulation and, with it, innovations proceed at a pace fast enough to overbear the retarding effect of population growth, the economy progresses. If it does not, the economy stagnates.

Here there is a parting of ways. Adam Smith envisages a progressive economy with his eyes fixed on technological innovations and division of labour, while Ricardo is apparently depressed by the prospects of diminishing returns in agriculture, rising cost of labour and falling rate of profit.

Now, whatever the approach, the policy implication was the same. The market must be widened through free trade—on Adam Smith's argument because a wider market would offer greater scope for division of labour, while on Ricardo's because an extension of foreign trade, in so far as it facilitated the import of 'corn' would reduce wages and raise profits. Classical theory thus not only provided answers to the specific problems that England faced at the time, it also suggested policy prescriptions which played an important part in reorienting its economy to suit the circumstances. The economy needed free trade and Theory rationalized it.

The classical system evolved in a particular setting provided by the country of its origin, and it is often contended that its significance is confined to the limits of that particular setting. 'Classical theory flowered on the British soil; would it not wither elsewhere?' is a question which is very often asked. Because of its association with a policy which was found inappropriate in other countries with dissimilar conditions, classical theory itself became suspect. Now this is a mistake. It is not enough to show certain obvious limitations of the Torrens-Ricardo comparative cost theory—although even there, with slight modifications to allow for non-labour costs, the theory can perhaps be used as an 'explanatory hypothesis' in relation to a short period over which fundamental changes do not occur. As a guide to policy the theory undoubtedly is deceptive.

To get at the more significant element of the classical theory of foreign trade one must go further back to Adam Smith. In spite of its subsequent recognition as *the* classical theory, the doctrine of comparative costs just does not fit in with the general framework of classical economics. The doctrine of comparative costs is based on a static, 'constant return' assumption, whereas classical economics is moulded in a dynamic framework and does allow for increasing returns. Classical economics has suffered in prestige considerably on account of its apparent association with a doctrine which takes no account of the possibility of increasing returns. For you cannot properly explain the secular movement of international trade except in terms of increasing returns. Adam Smith perceived it. In his famous dictum—'Division of labour is limited by the extent of the market'—you have a proposition which is perfectly general, not only as an explanation of the phenomena of international trade but also as a guide to policy.[1] Consider a country which exhibits conditions

[1] Professor J. R. Hicks, who certainly could not be accused of being unsympathetic to Ricardian Economics, goes to the length of saying in one of his recent essays: 'It is impossible to make sense of the phenomena of international trade unless one lays great stress upon *increasing returns*; and this is particularly important, because of the close connection between increasing returns and accumulation of capital.' (*Essays* in *World Economics*: Oxford, 1959, p. 183.) It is as if Adam Smith is speaking—for what else is 'division of labour' but a

unlike those that the classical economists postulated—a country big in size, exporting 'corn' and importing manufactures. Here it is the presence of foreign trade—the import of low cost manufactures—that limits the scope of division of labour. For such a country the policy prescription that emerges from the Smithian doctrine is Protection, not Free Trade. If 'theories are nets',[1] one must know how to cast, if one is to catch.

## II

Challenge to classical theory came not from 'outside', but from 'within'—not from the Historical School nor from the Socialists, but from the Marginalists. The socialists, including Karl Marx, built on classical theory, while the Historical School repudiated theory altogether. It is the Marginalists who diverted economic theory away from the main stream, concentrating chiefly on value and resource allocation. And even here it was no longer a problem of variations in absolute values over time and their impact upon society but a problem of 'relative prices' seen as functioning within the framework of an impersonal, self-adjusting economic system. So pronounced was this deviation that with the emergence of marginalism the problems that evoked classical economics came very nearly to be forgotten. It is only in recent years, partly under the impact of post-Keynesian 'growth' economics and partly due to the urgency created by a more intimate appreciation of the problem of what Myrdal calls 'international economic integration' that the older sights are reappearing.

The advent of marginalism did indeed mark a revolution in economic theory. The old terms no doubt continue to be used, but they have lost their old connotation. Not only is a new technique introduced into economic analysis, but the structure and content of economic theory have also received a new orientation. Value has ceased to be an absolute, measurable entity; it has become a ratio of exchange, without a dimension.[2] Distribution appears as an extension of the theory of value—being just a problem of pricing of factors of production. The two aspects of the economic problem are then integrated into a unified and logically self-consistent system. The old tripartite division of 'factors' into land, labour and capital is retained, but their old association with social 'classes' (or 'orders of society',

medium for the operation of Increasing Returns? One should, however, be careful not to confuse this with Torrens' 'territorial division of labour', which is another name for comparative costs and which only refers to 'allocation of resources', not to 'technique' of production.

[1] Popper: *The Logic of Scientific Discovery* (London, 1959), Chapter III, p. 59.

[2] See Jevons: *The Theory of Political Economy* (London, 4th edition, 1911), p. 83.

as Adam Smith would put it) is lost. Factors are conceived just as productive agents independently of the institutional framework within which they operate. The concepts of Cost and Surplus thus cease to have the significance that they acquired in classical political economy. Cost stands for 'opportunity surrendered', and Surplus turns out to be an excess of the actual income of a factor over its transfer price. Whereas in the classical system these concepts were used as criteria for the evaluation of the economic progress of a society—indeed the labour theory of value derives whatever significance it has from just this consideration, in the new system they are used as criteria for judging allocative efficiency, their application being confined primarily to the sphere of taxation.

The marginal technique was designed to bring out the principle of maximization that is supposed to characterize rational conduct. In the equation of the price ratio of goods with their marginal utility ratio there is the fulfilment of maximum principle in respect of consumer's expenditure. And in the equation of the price ratio of factors with the marginal productivity ratio we have a similar fulfilment of maximum principle in respect of the firm's choice of technique of production. Precisely the same principle is postulated in respect of the allocation of resources where it expresses itself in an equation between the price ratio and marginal cost ratio of products.

The entire analysis proceeds on the basis of the principle of substitution. Economic phenomena are manifestations of choice exercised by consumers and producers in respect of the disposal of scarce resources, and the phenomenon of choice in human behaviour is inseparably associated with the phenomenon of substitution. The principle of choice and substitution is thus fundamental in the marginalist system of economic theory. The system is worked out within the framework of a static economy—population, tastes, technology and resources being all held as data. This surely is in sharp contrast with the classical approach which is set out against the background of a growing economy, where the dynamic determinants such as accumulation of capital, technical progress and growth of population are shown as integral parts of the analytical model. How pronounced the cleavage is between the two systems is seen from the fact that whereas Adam Smith's enquiry was into the nature and causes of the Wealth of Nations, one of the modern exponents of the marginalist system goes to the length of urging that 'in strict delimitation of economic science' the term Wealth should be discarded.[1]

It must be a puzzle to the historian of economic thought how economic theory should have taken such a sharp turn away from the

[1] Lionel Robbins, *The Nature and Significance of Economic Science* (London 2nd edition, 1935), Chapter III, p. 47 n.

classical direction and why the initiative should have come at the same time from three different centres, as it did.

The sociology of scientific discovery is a complicated subject, and no single explanation of the phenomenon would perhaps be deemed adequate. Shift of events could hardly explain it. It is not the Ricardian 'stationary state' into which the new technique was projected, although it is there that it legitimately belongs. In fact, if economic events were the determining factor, we might have in the post-classical period a theory of crisis rather than a theory of static equilibrium. For as sequel to the industrial revolution, the countries of the West had already started experiencing the 'paradox of poverty in plenty' and the period 1873–98 during which the marginalist school established itself was marked by a slump so conspicuous as to have earned the title Great Depression.

One would perhaps be inclined to put the emergence of the marginal principle as an instance of 'pure reason'; indeed there is something in the analytic vision displayed in the system of at least one of the leaders of the school—Walras—which lends strong support to this view. Here too one would find it difficult to explain why different centres could have seen the same light at the same time. Nor is it easy to see what made it possible for the new doctrine to get so readily absorbed in the corpus of economic theory. Others had seen the light before—Lloyd and Dupuit and Gossen, for example—and they went into wilderness. Jevons, Menger and Walras, on the other hand, just 'came and conquered'.

The discovery (or, as one would prefer to say, rediscovery) of the marginal utility principle and the associated development of economic theory could not surely be an isolated scientific phenomenon. There must have been some sort of provocation somewhere. And one cannot help suspecting that the provocation was largely political; the connexion between the emergence of the marginal utility school and the political side of the teachings of Karl Marx seems to be too close to be ignored. Marginalism came up, so to say, to 'save' economic theory from being turned into an engine of class-war. In breaking away from Classical Political Economy it bid fair to destroy the theoretical foundation of the *Communist Manifesto*. In the theory of Exchange and Distribution, the Marginalist School offered an alternative explanation of social relations which cut across 'classes' and was designed as a counter to Marxist political propaganda. The switchover from 'accumulation' to 'consumption' as the mainspring of economic activity, the principle of maximization in the analysis of consumer's behaviour, the consistency theorem relating to individual maxima in the analysis of equilibrium of exchange, the marginal productivity principle of distribution, the application of Euler's theorem to the solution of the so-called 'adding up' problem

—implicit in all these is one long refutation of the Marxist theory of class-war and a plea for economic liberalism. If the marginalists were anti-classical[1] in their economic theorizing, they were overwhelmingly classical in their political predilections.[2]

Now, whatever may be the impulse that stimulated the discovery of the marginal utility principle, there can be little doubt about its significance for the development of economic theory. For over sixty years since the marginalist revolution, economists have kept busy refining and sharpening the technique of analysis which it opened up, and within its limited frame of reference, the technique has yielded significant results. Our knowledge of the nature of equilibrium of exchange is much more precise now than it was even thirty years ago. We now know better what elements constitute the theory of demand; one may refer to the separation of the income effect from the substitution effect of price variation, which is not merely a contribution of utmost importance to economic theory, but is also a valuable aid to econometric studies. The conditions of stability of interrelated markets are now capable of being more precisely shown, and we have a better analysis of the working of forces needed to bring back the equilibrium of an economic system once it is disturbed—the system consisting not only of commodities and factors but also of securities. The technique of deriving welfare propositions is also more scientific today, and we know better their significance as well as limitations for economic policy. It is said that the more advanced a theory is, the less is the use of 'data' and more the use of 'inference' that it involves. Judged by this test, the advance in economic theory that marginalism has led to is considerable.

True—but all this advance is within the framework of an economy with given 'tastes and obstacles'. Once we get into the dynamic field—where 'tastes and obstacles' are themselves a function of the rate of exchange, the analysis goes awry.

Let us see what it all means. Let us take the simple case of exchange between two persons in respect of two goods—the famous barter case of Alfred Marshall.[3] We know that in this case the rate of exchange ('terms of trade', as some of you might prefer to call it) would lie between the limits set by the zero-indifference curves of the trading parties or, in case the goods are 'produced', by their comparative costs. Now, if these outer limits are given—if, that is to say, the 'tastes and obstacles' are constant, you can chalk out a path from any point on the so-called contract curve which would lead the trading parties to a determinate rate of exchange, on the simple

[1] Cf. Jevons' vitriolic remark: '. . . that able but wrong headed man, David Ricardo, shunted the car of economic science on to a wrong line . . .' ibid., p. li.

[2] Is it because of this latter affiliation that they are often described as 'neo-classical'?

[3] Marshall, *Principles of Economics* (London, 7th edition, 1916), Appendix F.

assumption that successive transactions enable the parties gradually to acquire knowledge of their respective preference systems.[1] However, suppose that the tastes and obstacles are themselves a function of the rate of exchange; the outer limits may then recede in a direction unfavourable to the weaker party, and *this recession may proceed cumulatively until the limit of tolerance is reached.*

Now this has awkward consequences for equilibrium theory. For, the simple case just considered typifies the entire universe with which equilibrium theory is concerned. Indeterminateness prevades the whole field of exchange—between persons, between groups, between sectors and between nations. 'The whole creation groans' exclaims Edgeworth, as he perceives this ubiquity of indeterminateness, and he seeks relief in arbitration.[2] Static analysis glosses over the awkward edges of economic theory by invoking such devices as the law of indifference, crying of prices, recontract etc. And in terms of these devices a *possible* equilibrium is constructed. But paradoxically the construction that is drawn turns out to be not so much an aid to the interpretation of reality as a model for short term planning of resource allocation. The dynamics of exchange—which is what reality is—reveals, on the other hand, disharmony, if not conflict. In a situation where the so-called data of static theory are themselves determinates of the system, the weaker party (be it a 'class', a 'sector' or a 'nation') is apt to find its position cumulatively deteriorating in the process of exchange.[3]

So we are brought back to just where we left off Karl Marx. A certain disharmony is inherent in exchange relations as they operate through the market. Whether, however, the disharmony is inevitably resolved by 'war', as Marx would have it, or it lends itself to treatment by 'countervailing power', 'arbitration' or 'pact' is another matter. For that depends, one might say, upon the degree of sanity and resourcefulness that the world concerned is endowed with at a given stage of its civilization.

## III

While our economists were developing a 'method of analysis' by reference back to the choice of individuals to exhibit the properties

[1] See my 'A Note on the Determinateness of Equilibrium', *The Economic Journal*, September, 1954; also 'The Use of Curves in the Analysis of Market Price', *Indian Economic Journal*, July, 1954, reproduced below.

[2] 'Throughout the whole region of in a wide sense *contract*, in the general absence of a mechanism like perfect competition, the same essential indeterminateness prevails . . . The whole creation groans and yearns, desiderating a principle of arbitration, an end of strife.' Edgeworth, *Mathematical Psychics* (London School Reprint), p. 51.

[3] For an application of the dynamics of exchange to the labour market, see Marshall, ibid., Book VI, Chapter IV, Sec. 6.

of Economy and Waste, the 'subject matter' of Economics—Wealth and Poverty—slipped into the background.[1] Now it is this latter—the production and distribution of wealth and the social relations that they engender that was the preoccupation of the classical economists from Adam Smith down to, shall I say, Karl Marx. For, with all the mysticisms and terminological vagaries that shroud the analytic content of *Das Kapital,* was not Marx, the economic theorist, a disciple of Smith and Ricardo? The canvas that Marx uses is undoubtedly of a bigger dimension—for he takes institutions, too, as a determinate of the system and not just a datum, as Smith or Ricardo did. But in respect of the type of *economic* questions that he asks and in respect of the mode that he adopts in answering them he was indeed very much of a 'classical'.

It took long for us to recognize this. Even twenty-five years ago in the orthodox circle Marx would be mentioned only to be criticized. Now, while particular aspects of Marxian economics could be made an easy target by a clever marksman, the core of his theory which relates to economic development and crisis still stands and is reflected in what one might call Modern Economics. The cycle is complete, and we are now again asking very much the same type of questions as concerned Marx and we seem to be seeking answers very much in the same way as he did.

Thanks to the awareness concerning the state of stagnation of capital-saturated 'advanced' economies on the one hand and of capital-hungry 'stunted' economies on the other, Growth has again assumed the central position in economic theory. The former is a follow-up of the Keynesian theory of under-employment equilibrium and leads up to models of steady growth. The latter is a problem of 'primary accumulation' and leads up to models of accelerated growth. These are the problems on which Modern Economics is focusing attention. And they are essentially Marxian problems. The apparatus that is being used today for the analysis of the problems has also a family resemblance to the Marxian apparatus, couched as it might often be in a different language. You have the old emphasis on accumulation as the prime mover of the economic system and on surplus as the source of accumulation. You have also the division of the economy into 'sectors' and the typical Marxian way of setting out equilibrium conditions in terms of inter-sectoral balance—only you now have more sectors than Marx contemplated. Again, as in the Marxian system, consumption has come to be relegated to a subsidiary position and shown primarily as a function of the rate of

[1] For an exposition of the two aspects of Economics—'method' and 'subject-matter', see an illuminating paper by J. R. Hicks on 'Economic Theory and Social Sciences' published in a volume entitled *The Social Sciences: Their Relations in Theory and in Teaching* (Le Play House, London, 1936).

accumulation. The concepts of 'unlimited supply of labour', 'disguised unemployment', 'saving potential' and so on that are today being so widely used in growth models in the context of underdeveloped economies are reminiscent of Marx's theory of primary accumulation.[1] Towards the close of the last century—within thirty years of the appearance of *Das Kapital*, Bohm-Bawerk, one of the leaders of the Marginalist School, wrote a book which he called *Karl Marx and the Close of His System*.[2] The centenary of *Das Kapital* is soon coming; who knows ere it comes someone will not come with a companion volume—*Karl Marx and the Revival of His System*.

Indeed the pendulum has swung the other way, and we seldom hear nowadays of market-forms and prices. In the broad perspective that we are taking, it appears as though Marginalism came as a sort of an interlude in the development of economic theory. And if the explanation of the advent of Marginalism that I was suggesting has at all any validity, one may well wonder what the course of economic theory would have been had Marx shed his propaganda and remained the good classical economist that he really was.

Yet having got so far with the theory of relative prices, is it not tempting to see where is stands in relation to the theory of growth? You cannot just throw the marginalist system overboard—for it does answer such questions as it raises more satisfactorily than does classical political economy. It does offer a more general theory of resource allocation, subsuming the classical labour theory as a special case. Witness, in contrast, the impasse that Marx creates by undertaking the impossible task of integrating the theory of relative prices into the labour theory of value. Surely the marginalist theory of relative prices and resource allocation with its emphasis on scarcity and choice has made its place in the general corpus of economic science.

Where, then, is the junction between these two strands of economic theory—the theory of relative prices and the theory of growth? The two theories have so far taken shape independently—often indeed at cross purposes. There is, however, no obvious reason why it should have been so. The economic universe, both in its static aspect and in its dynamic aspect, is the resultant of the process of allocation of

[1] Compare, e.g. the following passage: 'Although the number of the tillers of the soil was decreased, the land produced as much fruit as before . . . When, therefore, part of the rural population was set free from the land, the means of subsistence with which they had been nourished as landworkers were likewise set free. Such means of subsistence were transformed into the material elements of variable capital.' Karl Marx, *Capital* (Everyman's Library), p. 826.

[2] The original German edition of the book was published in 1896; the English translation came out in 1898. The interpretation adopted here is what the English title would suggest. See, however, Paul Sweezy's remarks in his own edition of the book (New York, 1949), Editor's Introduction, p. vi.

resources operating through relative prices. When gross investment is just equal to depreciation, the significant problem turns out to be the horizontal allocation of resources—the problem *par excellence* of static analysis. When, however, gross investment exceeds depreciation, so that net investment is positive the vertical allocation of resources also assumes importance. And it is this vertical allocation operating through the rate of interest that determines the rate of growth.

This, however, is only the beginning of the problem of economic dynamics. For net investment leads to the formation of capital, and the form that the new capital takes on sets the pattern of future growth, and the process goes on *irreversibly*, with the distinction between data and determinates obliterated, as in the case of simple exchange set out earlier.

How do relative prices behave in this process of continuous growth, and in what way does the marginalist analysis of price fit in with the framework of long-run movement? What are the functions that relative prices perform in a continuously growing economy? How is growth in its turn, and technical progress that accompanies it, affected by a given system of relative prices? These are the sorts of questions that a dynamic theory will have to answer, and one is tempted to suggest that it is in the search for an answer to such questions—in the construction of a synthesis, that is, between the theory of value and the theory of growth that the future development of economic theory will lie.

The relation between relative prices and economic growth is a two-way relation. Within any given environmental setting, the system of relative prices no doubt determines the rate of growth through its effect upon accumulation and the technique of production. Yet growth also in its turn does react on the system of relative prices via the pattern of investment and distribution of income.

So long as an economy can depend on entrepreneurship to usher in innovations and, within the framework of these innovations, to undertake investments adequate enough to secure a rate of growth such as would be warranted by the growth of population and labour supply, one could leave the problem of growth alone and concentrate on relative prices. For it is these relative prices that are of immediate concern to individuals and groups. This is true of an economy which is in the 'adult' stage of its career and does not suffer either from capital saturation or from capital shortage. The major economic problem of such an economy is to be able to retain what it has already acquired by avoiding misdirection of resources and consequent waste. The age and environment of the Marginalists conform fairly closely to this description. In the Keynesian world of advanced economies, on the other hand, where accumulation is retarded by deficiency of effective demand, the problem of growth takes on a special significance, if only because a minimum of it is essential for the maintenance of a reasonable level of employment. Relative prices may in such an economy be left alone, to be determined by the required rate of growth. But for an economy whose progress has been historically stifled by the shortage of capital and entrepreneurship and which is marked by mass poverty, the problem is more complicated. While growth must be recognized here also as the governing force, relative prices cannot just be left alone to take their own course, nor can the allocation of resources be left to be regulated by the movement of relative prices, as the principle of economic liberalism would dictate. You cannot permit a natural development of the price system and the corresponding pattern of resource allocation *consistently* with the required rate of growth in such an economy; forced pace of growth that the economy needs must inevitably be accompanied by control and direction of the price system as also of the allocation of resources.

# 2

# KEYNESIAN ECONOMICS AND UNDER-DEVELOPED COUNTRIES*

## I

The propositions of Keynes's *General Theory* are by now well known. I would, however, restate them in a slightly different order, placing emphasis on certain ingredients and bringing out one or two implicit assumptions which are relevant to the present enquiry.

Let me start with the definition of 'full employment', from which is derived the core of Keynesian economics—the concept of involuntary unemployment. Full employment signifies a state in which any person *willing* to work at a wage rate that corresponds to his economic contribution to the product of the industry, finds a job at that wage. To put it in more precise terms, in a state of full employment, the marginal unit of labour gets a wage in real terms, the utility derived from which is equal to the disutility that the work involves. From this it follows that in a state of involuntary unemployment the utility of wage exceeds the marginal disutility of labour. 'Men are involuntarily unemployed if, in the event of a small rise in the price of wage-goods relatively to the money wage, both the aggregate supply of labour willing to work for the current money-wage and the aggregate demand for it at that wage would be greater than the existing volume of employment.'[1]

Keynes does not offer an independent theory of wages. He accepts the ordinary theory that the 'real' wage rate is equated in equilibrium to the marginal productivity of labour. But—and this is important—he emphasizes that real wage is a derived concept and does not in itself represent the terms on which wage bargains are made. The wage bargain in the market runs in money terms, and the real wage rate is derived from the money wage rate relative to the prices of wage-goods.

The period of reference is a 'short period' over which, among other things, capital equipment and technique are given and constant, these being the result of past investment. Labour is employed upon a given capital equipment, and is pushed up to the 'margin of profit-

* Summary of a course of extension lectures which the author delivered under the auspices of the University of Lucknow in the autumn of 1949. An earlier version was published in *The Economic Weekly*, Independence Number, January 26, 1954.

[1] Keynes, *The General Theory of Employment, Interest and Money* (London, 1936), p. 15. The sentence is in italics in the text.

ableness'. A short period equilibrium is thus envisaged for the economy as a whole. However, although Keynes's analysis runs in terms of a short period, it does not preclude longer-run inferences. For a long period is a succession of short periods, each endowed with a different capital equipment and carrying the legacy of the past.[1]

Propositions supporting the Keynesian theory of involuntary unemployment can now be set forth.

(i) Money wage rate is fixed more or less conventionally between employers and trade unions. This given money wage rate provides the measure of the magnitudes involved in the analysis. Consumption, investment, prices etc., are measured in terms of 'wage-unit', i.e. the money wage received by a representative unit of labour.[2]

(ii) Prices of wage-goods, along with the general price level, are determined by the expenditure on consumption and investment.

(iii) Expenditure on consumption goods is limited, with reference to a given prospective income, by the extent to which income earners are inclined to spend rather than to save.

(iv) Expenditure on investment is limited, given the market rate of interest, by the prospective marginal net yield of investment.

(v) A decision not to spend on consumption does not necessarily mean a decision to invest; the rate of interest which is ordinarily supposed to be the connecting link between the two is determined not just by the propensity to save but by the preference of the people to hold cash.

(vi) The expenditure on consumption and the expenditure on investment, between them, make up the aggregate demand price of output as a whole, and short period equilibrium is struck at a point where the aggregate demand price is equated to the aggregate supply price.

(vii) Under conditions of equilibrium, therefore, the price level may be too low relatively to the given money wage rate, or, in other words, the real wage rate may be too high for full employment to be secured. More than full employment can be

[1] It is important not to miss this. For it provides the basis of the famous stagnation thesis. If—to anticipate our story—the 'marginal efficiency of capital' depends at all upon the stock of capital existing currently, then, in the absence of favourable exogenous factors, such as innovation, growth of markets, etc., every act of new investment over a given period creates difficulties for the next period by enlarging the capital equipment and lowering its prospective yield. However, I shall have occasion in a later section to refer to this matter, for, as I feel, so far as this longer-run aspect of Keynes's theory is concerned, the conditions of under-developed economies are in sharp contrast with those of mature economies.

[2] Note the family resemblance between Keynes's 'wage-unit' and the 'labour command measure' of Adam Smith and Malthus.

ruled out, for the workers have the option not to work if the real wage rate fails to compensate for the disutility of labour. But less than full employment is a probability; indeed it tends to be a normal feature of an economy which suffers from a low marginal propensity to consume and a low marginal efficiency of capital.

(viii) The unemployment that emerges is 'involuntary' when it is found either (a) that the labourers, being under a 'money illusion', are prepared to put up with a higher price level, even though they are unwilling to accept a cut in money wage rate, or (b) that even with a cut in money wage rate, it is not possible to effect a reduction in the real wage rate. For, in either case, while the labourers are willing to accept a lower rate of real wage at which employers also find it worth while offering more employment, the mechanism by which this could be effected is absent, unless special measures are taken.

(ix) These special measures include: (a) transference of income from the relatively rich to the relatively poor—thus causing a tendency to an increase in the propensity to consume; (b) maintenance of a low rate of interest as an inducement for larger investment. The potency of these measures is, however, limited. A tax on higher incomes, in so far as it touches profits, would prejudice private investment. On the other hand, the effectiveness of interest policy is dubious, if only because the liquidity preference of the people being what it is, there is a limit below which the rate of interest cannot be brought down. Hence what is indicated is a more direct measure, namely public investment through deficit finance, unprofitable as it may appear at first sight. A dose of public investment, in so far as it is not at the expense of private investment, would release forces making for increased consumption, whereby the increment of aggregate output will be a multiple of the initial investment, the value of the multiplier depending upon the marginal propensity to consume.[1]

This is Keynes's General Theory in its pristine form. I have tried to bring out the essentials of the theory and to put it in a form which makes it inevitable that any pushing up of employment should be accompanied by a reduction in the *real* rate of wages. And of course

[1] Students of Pigou's *Economics of Welfare* will notice that, in the context of involuntary unemployment, the multiplier formula provides yet another conspicuous example of a discrepancy between marginal private net product and marginal social net product. Equilibrium, as reflected in the equation between the marginal efficiency of capital and the current rate of interest, implies that an additional dose of investment by itself is unprofitable and would not be undertaken in the private sector. But when the secondary repercussions touching the various consumption goods industries are taken into account, the investment turns out to be *socially* profitable and hence it is to be undertaken by the state.

this is what Keynes had in mind; the hypothesis is one of diminishing returns at or near full employment. 'Thus *if* employment increases, then, in the short period, the reward per unit of labour in terms of wage-goods must, in general decline and profits increase.'[1] This, indeed, as Keynes takes care to point out, is one of the postulates of classical theory with which his own analysis is in accord.

## II

Now, one who is acquainted with the conditions of an under-developed economy,[2] with the earnings of the majority of the working population practically below the minimum subsistence level, will find it hard to see how the prevailing real wage in these economies could be too high. He will surely look askance at Keynes's theory of involuntary unemployment, and perhaps on this ground alone would throw it overboard. However, let us look at the matter a little more closely.

It should be obvious from a scrutiny of the constituents of Keynesian economics, as enumerated above, that they pertain to an economy in which 'money' serves as the instrument of economic operations, in which these operations include borrowing and lending, and in which, further, the ownership of the means of production is divorced from the use of these means, which is to say that labour is divorced from capital. Wherever these conditions prevail, Keynesian technique of analysis applies. And these conditions are the conditions of capitalism in that special sense in which the socialists use the term.[3] It is under capitalism that savers are distinct from investors, that net profit is the motive force behind production and employment, and that wage rate is determined in money as a result of a bargain between two parties—the employers and the employed.

To what extent are these characteristics present in the so-called under-developed economies? Even in India which, in respect of the stage of economic development—though not in respect of *per capita* income—happens to be the most advanced among the under-developed countries of South-East Asia, it is only over a small field that these conditions hold good. The organized sector of our economy, with its large scale industries and a fairly well-developed

[1] Keynes, *General Theory*, p. 17. This consideration disposes of one possible comment on Keynes's *General Theory*, namely that, in its preoccupation with the employment of labour, it neglects the implication of the existence of other kinds of idle resources. For, to say that capital equipment is worked beyond the stage of diminishing returns is another way of saying that it is fully employed. Full employment of labour in Keynes's model, does indeed imply full employment of capital.

[2] The characteristics of an under-developed economy will unfold themselves as we proceed. No precise definition is attempted here.

[3] Cf. R. F. Harrod, *The Trade Cycle* (Oxford, 1936), pp. 23–35.

banking system, does no doubt come under the scope of Keynesian economics, for it presents features no less 'capitalistic' than those associated with the so-called advanced economies. But the place that this sector occupies in the national economy from the point of view of its contribution to employment (as distinct from its contribution to income) is surely insignificant. The waste due to 'involuntary unemployment', if there is any, in this sector is surely of the second order of smalls, when considered in relation to the total working population of the country. Assuming, for example, that persons involuntarily unemployed constitute 10 per cent of the number actually employed in organized industry, and assuming further that organized industry absorbs 2 per cent of the total working population (these are hypothetical figures, but not far outside the mark), we find that involuntary unemployment turns out to be just 0·2 per cent of the total working population. Reliable unemployment figures for the South Asian countries are not available. However, the following table showing the waste due to unemployment in certain western countries is revealing.

*Average Income per head of Working Population in International Units, 1925–34*[1]

| | *Employed and Unemployed taken together* | *Approximate estimate if all Unemployed had been at work* |
|---|---|---|
| USA | 1368 | 1550 |
| Canada | 1337 | 1440 |
| Great Britain | 1089 | 1210 |
| Sweden | 653 | 700 |
| France | 694 | 720 |
| Germany | 646 | 750 |
| Norway | 539 | 590 |
| Austria | 511 | 570 |
| Czechoslovakia | 455 | 480 |
| Italy | 343 | 363 |

The figures in the table are based on the most generous assumption, namely that the average productivity of the unemployed would have been about the same as those who were actually in work if the unemployed had been absorbed in industry. Yet, barring USA, Great Britain and Germany—countries which are definitely the more capitalistic in our sense—the waste due to unemployment during a period which includes years of one of the severest depressions known in history is surprisingly small.

[1] Colin Clark, *Conditions of Economic Progress* (1st edition, London, 1940), p. 77.

## III

The fact is that a large part of the economy of the under-developed countries does not come under money transactions at all, and even where it does, in so far as the organization of the industry is such that the worker works with his own tools (e.g. cottage industries), the level of activity is determined by considerations of gross income and not of net profit. The conditions in these sectors conform closely to those of Crusoe economy where the level of activity is within the control of the workers themselves and where, therefore, Harrod's prime determinants—viz, Diminishing Utility of Commodities, Increasing Dis-utility of Work and Diminishing Returns—function in their pristine form.[1] All this explains why in India, for example, the depression of the thirties did not affect employment so much as it did prices, and why, on the other hand, the stimulus to investment during the last war was almost immediately followed by inflation and a rise in money wages.

The possibility of involuntary unemployment is not denied, in so far as even an under-developed economy may contain an organized sector wherein the Keynesian propositions hold good. But its magnitude is not likely to be appreciable, if only because the marginal propensity to consume in a low level economy, despite large inequalities of income, tends to be relatively high; and, although investment opportunities are limited, yet, when account is taken of the fact that most of these economies are characterized by a rapidly growing population, they should not normally lag behind the rate at which people are inclined to save. Indeed, whatever the generality of the *General Theory* may be in the sense in which the term 'general' was used by Keynes,[2] the applicability of the propositions of the General Theory to conditions of an under-developed economy is at best limited.

Keynes makes liquidity preference the villain in his diagnosis of the stagnation of an under-developed economy 'The history of India,' he says, 'at all times has provided an example of a country impoverished by a preference for liquidity amounting to so strong a passion that even an enormous and chronic influx of the precious metals has been insufficient to bring down the rate of interest to a level which was compatible with the growth of real wealth.'[3] The levelling down of the structure of interest rates would surely be welcome in a country like India as a measure towards a better distribution of income. But it is doubtful, in spite of Keynes, if it

[1] Cf. Harrod, ibid., Chapter 1, pp. 1–11.

[2] The title *General Theory* was apparently used by Keynes to emphasize that the theory takes account of the possibility of under-employment equilibrium not envisaged by the so-called classical economists.

[3] *General Theory*, Chapter 23, p. 337. This passage happens to be a solitary reference in the *General Theory* to the problem of an under-developed economy.

would have any significant effect upon output and employment. The experience of the last war has taught us that the monetization of precious metals would, in the economic set-up of the country, work more towards a rise of prices than towards the 'growth of real wealth'; the operation of the multiplier would be swamped by a rise in money wages. The trouble in India at all times has been not that the influx of precious metals did not find expression in an increased supply of money—the absorption of precious metals into hoards at least kept up an export surplus for the country. The trouble has been, on the other hand, that the influx of precious metals was not replaced by imports of capital goods as such.

Paradoxically, in spite of growing population and shortage of capital relative to labour, India, as other under-developed economies, has at all times suffered from a low marginal efficiency of capital. The unhealthy preference for precious metals as against capital goods is to be attributed to this. The cause of a low marginal efficiency of capital in these economies, however, is to be sought not in the direction of Keynes but rather in the direction of J. B. Say. If the curve of marginal efficiency of capital has to be raised, what is needed is, as Rosenstein-Rodan has shown,[1] a simultaneous development of a unmber of industries the supply of goods in one creating demand for goods in others. And this involves an expansion in the aggregate stock of capital resources. The limiting factor in the growth of employment in an economy such as ours is not so much a shortage of money as a shortage of real capital. With the existing capital equipment, even if we have 'full employment' in the Keynesian sense, a large volume of unemployment will still remain in the physical sense. When capital equipment is low and population large, marginal productivity comes down to the level of the marginal disutility of labour at a stage where unemployment still persists in the physical sense, though not in the 'involuntary' sense. Our economists, misappropriating a term that Mrs Robinson uses in another context,[2] often call it 'disguised unemployment'. In fact, however, it is a phenomenon which is not connected in any way with a fall in effective demand, nor does it go along with excess capacity in capital resources. It is there because the maximum capacity of capital equipment is inadequate to fully employ the available labour.[3]

[1] P. N. Rosenstein-Rodan, 'Problems of Industrialisation in Eastern and South-eastern Europe', *The Economic Journal*, June–September, 1943. See also R. Nurkse, *Problems of Capital Formation in Under-developed Countries* (Oxford, 1953).

[2] Joan Robinson, *Essays in the Theory of Employment* (London, 1937), pp. 60–2.

[3] This, I take it, is the implication of the grim warning of M. Kalecki: 'If the maximum capacity of equipment is inadequate to absorb the available labour, as will be the case in backward countries, the immediate achievement of full employment is clearly hopeless.' *The Economics of Full Employment* (Oxford Institute of Statistics), p. 43.

This suggests a notion of shifting points of 'full employment' equilibrium. With each expansion of capital equipment, the marginal productivity of labour rises and, the disutility curve of labour remaining constant, we have a higher level of 'full employment'. The notion of an ascending level of 'full employment' emerges readily from the hypothesis that the potential marginal productivity of labour with reference to an increasing supply of capital resources is larger than the marginal productivity as it actually is. Capital saturation is marked by a stage where absence of involuntary unemployment ensures absence of unemployment in the physical sense, too, barring frictions due to lack of mobility of labour.

## IV

What happens in this background about the much talked-of stagnation theory? Will each expansion in the stock of capital lower the marginal efficiency of capital while it raises the marginal productivity of labour? Does expansion itself contain seeds of stagnation? The answer is again to be sought in Rodan's hypothesis. Capital saturation is a long way off for an under-developed economy with a strong pressure of population and a depressed standard of living. For such an economy, an increase of capital resources, if it could be brought about, will make possible a simultaneous development of industries and will have, through the operation of 'external' economies,[1] rather the effect of raising the marginal efficiency of capital. Indeed this points to a peculiar feature of an under-developed economy which distinguishes it fundamentally from a so-called mature economy.

Keynes's model is that of an economy in which the supply of labour is perfectly elastic at current money rate of wages; the model to which the economies of under-developed countries are a close approximation, is one in which the supply of labour is perfectly elastic at current *real* rate of wages. In Keynes's model surplus labour is accompanied by excess capacity in capital equipment; in under-developed economies reserve capacities are deficient, if not non-existent. Further, in those mature economies which provide the model for Keynes's analysis, since there exists a gap between current real rate of wages and the minimum standard of comfort and since, therefore, there is scope for a reduction of the real wage rate, a rise in prices at the diminishing return stage is (at least theoretically) consistent with constant money rate of wages. In

[1] The phrase is Marshallian but is here used in a wider sense than Marshall would have it. Marshall's 'external economies' are economies which are external to the firm but internal to the industry. Here the phrase is used in the sense of economies which are external to an individual industry and which arise out of the general development of the economy.

under-developed economies, on the other hand, the current real rate of wages even in the urban sector, not to speak of the rural sector, is about the minimum necessary for physical existence. These economies cannot, therefore, allow prices to rise and yet expect the money rate of wages to remain constant.

All this has an important bearing on policy. The need for public investment is urgent if the objective in the under-developed economies is to achieve a higher standard of living and increasing volume of employment. And, in the absence of an adequate flow of foreign capital and an adequate volume of public savings, deficit financing is also called for. But whereas, in mature economies, deficit financing is more or less innocuous and can be depended on, with the aid of the multiplier, to achieve the desired level of employment without any substantial rise of prices and with a constant money rate of wages, in under-developed economies where structural resistances are strong, deficit financing leads to inflationary pressures and a tendency to a rise in money wage rate, except in so far as the pattern of investment is such as increases output within the time lag between the earning of additional money income and its spending on consumption goods. In such economies, therefore, deficit financing has to be accompanied in the transition period (i.e. till the structure of capital equipment is matched with the extended structure of demand) by a system of controls very much on the lines of war-time controls. If money wage rates are to be kept constant, prices of wage-goods must not be allowed to rise. And if resources are to be prevented from shifting to non-essential industries, price control must be accompanied by capital issue control. And so on. Public investment may perhaps proceed in the under-developed countries without curtailment of current consumption, though not along with increasing consumption, as it could in mature economies. But we would be deceiving ourselves if we thought that the process could function within the framework of a liberal economy, such as Keynes sought so anxiously to preserve.

# 3

# ON THE ASSUMPTION OF UNLIMITED SUPPLY OF LABOUR*

Economists have very often worked with the assumption of an unlimited supply of labour. But the contexts in which the assumption has been used are not the same, and it should be perhaps made clear that they are not. There are at least four strands that one can distinguish in this connexion:

(i) The Ricardian wage theory based on the Malthusian law of population growth;
(ii) Marx's Industrial Reserve Army;
(iii) The Keynesian concept of involuntary unemployment; and
(iv) Disguised unemployment relating to an under-developed country.

Implicit in all these formulations is the idea that the wage rate is independent of the demand for labour, or, in other words, that the supply of labour is perfectly elastic. Formally they look alike but their contents are not the same. The object of this paper is to show wherein the differences lie and incidentally also to indicate the policy implications in one or two contexts.

## I

In the Ricardian system, there are two concepts of wages which need being distinguished. The wage rate with which Ricardo connects the profit rate is a rate which is conceived in terms of an 'invariable standard'. This wage rate—which he calls 'the natural price of labour'—tends to rise as accumulation proceeds, in spite of a corresponding growth of population. This is due to the operation of diminishing returns in agriculture which supplies the 'food and necessaries' of labour. With the natural progress of society characterized by growing accumulation and growing population, more of capital and labour is employed on a given stock of land; diminishing returns set in, and food and necessaries forming the chief items in the labourer's budget tend to become costlier, measured in terms of an invariable standard. Therefore the wage rate, measured in terms of the same standard, tends to rise. And this rising wage rate is accompanied by a falling rate of profit, in so far as it is not checked by improvements in agriculture.

* Originally published in *The Economic Weekly* (Bombay), Annual Number, January, 1958.

What happens, however, to wages in terms of 'food and necessaries'—'wage goods', as we call them, following Pigou? Here Ricardo introduces the concept of a constant wage rate. Labourers as a class have a certain definite conception of what constitutes their minimum subsistence. This no doubt 'varies at different times in the same country and differs materially in different countries'; yet, given the notion of a minimum standard, the wage rate, estimated in terms of goods as such, is independent of the accumulation of capital and hence independent of the demand for labour. As accumulation proceeds, the demand for labour increases. Temporarily, therefore, wages tend to rise, in so far as they are regulated by supply and demand. But as soon as this happens, population tends to grow, following the Malthusian law, and the supply of labour adjusts itself to demand in such a way that wages come down to the level of minimum subsistence. Here is a theory of wages which runs in terms of a perfectly elastic supply of labour. It is a theory which is based on the assumption of a rate of population growth having a tendency to adjust itself to the rate of accumulation. Chronic unemployment is ruled out, as also a shortage of labour relative to capital.

## II

Marx's wage theory is formally very much the same as Ricardo's, although its implications are fundamentally different. Value of labour power is equated, by definition, to the value of the means of subsistence necessary for the maintenance of the labourer, and it is then argued that the price of labour (the rate of wages, that is) tends to conform to the value of labour. Marx recognizes, as Ricardo does, that the nature and volume of goods that make up the subsistence of the labourer are themselves determined by the circumstances of a society. But with reference to a given stage of historical development, the minimum subsistence of labour is assumed to consist of a definite quantity of commodities. How, then, does it happen that the rate of wages tends to conform to this minimum subsistence? Marx explains this not in terms of a law of population growth, as Ricardo does—indeed he has scant regard for the Malthusian law—but in terms of what he calls 'the reserve army of labour'.

As soon as an economy leaves off the stage of primary accumulation, as soon, that is to say, as labour gets dissociated from capital and assumes the position of wage-earner to be employed by the capitalist, it becomes the business of the capitalist to keep down the rate of wages to subsistence level with a view to creating enough 'surplus' to maintain the rate of profit. With an unvarying wage-output ratio, the progress of accumulation carries with it the tendency to a falling rate of profits. This tendency can be suspended and the profit rate maintained if wages are prevented from rising with increasing productivity of labour consequent on accumulation. The capitalist does it by resorting to one or the other of the following methods:

(a) varying the rate of accumulation;
(b) introducing technical improvements so as to substitute capital for labour; and
(c) creating monopoly power to suppress the demand for higher wages.

Any of these methods leads to the creation of an industrial reserve army. An army of unemployed labourers is kept floating, so to speak, in the economy—to be drawn upon as need arises, without any pressure for an upward revision of the wage rate. Chronic unemployment is what keeps the wage rate down to the level of minimum subsistence, and it is this feature of a capitalist economy that renders the supply of labour perfectly elastic.

## III

Keynes's theory of 'involuntary unemployment', too, leads up to a notion of constant wage rate. And formally, at any rate, it bears a close affinity to the Marxian theory of 'industrial reserve army', so much so that Mrs Robinson, referring in particular to this part of Keynesian theory, observes that 'recent developments in academic theory have led them [academic economists] to a position which in some respects resembles the position of Marx far more closely than the position of their own intellectual forebears'.[1] Deficiency of effective demand gives rise to involuntary unemployment which happens to be a chronic feature of a capitalist economy, particularly in its advanced stage. And in so far as the economy maintains a pool of unemployed labourers, an increase in effective demand results in an increase in the volume of employment; it does not affect the wage rate. The supply of labour is thus perfectly elastic till the economy attains 'full employment'. Put in this way, the proposition looks like the Marxian proposition based on the reserve army of labour. But the likeness is more apparent than real. The differences are fundamental.

First, the wage rate to which Keynes relates the supply of labour is the money wage rate and not the real wage rate. For institutional reasons, the money wage rate is supposed to be rigid, and it is at the current money wage rate that the supply of labour is supposed to be perfectly elastic under under-employment conditions. The real wage rate is equated to the marginal product of labour with reference to any given volume of employment, and its behaviour is determined

[1] Joan Robinson, *An Essay on Marxian Economics* (London, 1942), p. 5.

by the prices of wage-goods relative to the money wage rate. Indeed Keynes takes pains to show—and it is here that he departs fundamentally from his predecessors, including the neo-classicals—that there is no necessary connexion between the movement of money wages and the movement of real wages.

Secondly, the goods content of money wages is not equated in Keynes's system, as it is in the Marxian system, to the minimum subsistence of the labourer. Far from that. The implication of Keynes's theory is that the real wage rate is higher than the supply price of labour. The definition of 'involuntary unemployment' itself suggests this. And the policy prescription that Keynes provides as a possible cure for unemployment, namely, deficit-financing, can carry meaning only when the under-employment equilibrium which he postulates is one at which the real wage rate exceeds the minimum subsistence of the labourer, there being scope, consistently with the labourer's tolerance limit, for its reduction through higher prices of wage-goods. For, if the real wage rate were at the level of minimum subsistence, deficit-financing, in so far as it raised the prices of wage-goods, would automatically lead to a rise in money wages, thus frustrating the multiplier effect on which Keynes's policy prescription rests.

## IV

Here is the essential point of difference between Keynes's involuntary unemployment and 'disguised unemployment' as applied to an under-developed economy. Originally, no doubt, 'disguised unemployment' was conceived by Mrs Robinson as an extension of the Keynesian concept of involuntary unemployment. 'Thus a decline in demand for the product of the general run of industries leads to a diversion of labour from occupations in which productivity is higher to others where it is lower. The cause of this diversion, a decline in effective demand, is exactly the same as the cause of unemployment in the ordinary sense, and it is natural to describe the adoption of inferior occupations by dismissed workers as *disguised unemployment*.'[1] In the context of an under-developed economy, however, the concept of 'disguised unemployment' takes on a distinct property. As applied there, it is to be explained not in terms of a 'decline in effective demand' but in terms of a shortage of capital relative to the current size of population. In the rural sector, there is surplus labour pressing on a limited stock of land. And since the mode of production is family-oriented and pre-capitalistic, the labourer enjoys a living which is set by average productivity, even though the marginal productivity may turn out to be zero.

[1] Joan Robinson, *Essays in the Theory of Employment* (London, 1937), p. 62.

On the other hand, there is not enough outlet for this surplus labour in the urban sector where shortage of capital is already depressing the real wage rate down to the subsistence level of workers.

We have thus the spectacle of an 'unlimited supply of labour' at current real wage rate which is too low to permit a cut without impairing the efficiency of labour. The situation calls for an accelerated rate of investment towards capital formation. The additional investment, however, has to be financed, as far as possible, by additional savings, contrary to Keynes's prescription. Deficit-financing, in so far as it is not adequately matched by increased output of wage-goods, tends to raise the prices of wage-goods. And if this happens, there are two alternatives open to the economy, neither of which is palatable. It may keep the money wage rate constant, in which case the real wage rate comes down below the permissible level. Alternatively, it may keep the real wage rate constant and let money wages rise, in which case it opens the door to an inflationary spiral. It cannot too often be repeated, therefore, that if in such economies deficit-financing is to be resorted to beyond the safety limit provided by the price index of wage-goods, the state must not hesitate to adopt the policy of price control and rationing, be it a little anti-liberal.

# 4

# DISGUISED UNEMPLOYMENT AND ECONOMIC DEVELOPMENT*

## I

One of the distinctive features of an under-developed economy is the prevalence of what our economists are now in the habit of calling 'disguised unemployment'. Too many people subsist on agriculture. Seemingly they are employed. But their employment is not wholly productive. It is not wholly productive in the sense that production does not suffer even if some of the so-called employed are withdrawn. The ratio of labour to land and other resources is so large that the marginal productivity of labour is reduced to zero, although the average productivity remains positive. And, unlike in the organized sector, it is this average productivity and not the marginal productivity that determines the earnings, and hence consumption of the labourers. The result is that the marginal body of labourers consume, but they do not produce. They are employed physically, but not economically.

The organizational set-up (such as we have in a subsistence economy) is what makes for this. Farms consist of family holdings, and productive operations are done by the members of a family as a group. Labour is not dissociated from capital, and workers may be said to be self-employed. There are the landlords and the money-lenders. But they get their rent and interest at stipulated rates; they do not perform the function of an employer. Whatever output is derived from productive operations therefore vests in the family and is enjoyed by all the members irrespective of their specific contribution; the redundant members are not just thrown away. The share of output that goes to the redundant units of labour is of the nature of transfer income. If, of ten persons working in a farm, four are redundant, in the sense that the farm could be managed equally efficiently with six persons, then, from the economic point of view, 40 per cent of the output of the farm can be viewed as being transferred to unproductive consumers. It is as if the entire output is the contribution of six persons who just 'save' a part of this contribution and hand it over to the remaining four. Professor Nurkse calls this the 'saving potential' of a subsistence economy.

On this concept of 'saving potential' as a concomitant of 'disguised unemployment' C. N. Vakil and P. R. Brahmananda have built a

* Originally published in *The Economic Weekly*, August 25, 1956.

theory of economic growth.[1] Planning in an under-developed economy, if it is to be effective, must, according to our authors, take account of 'disguised unemployment' of the subsistence sector and make full use of the 'saving potential' that is associated with it. The process can be initiated only if the increase in the volume of employment in the planned sector is made to exceed the addition to the labour force consequent on the growth of population. So long as our plan seeks just to absorb the additional labour force that comes into the market as a result of population growth, the disguised unemployment remains untouched and with it the saving potential. Once, however, our planned investment passes this limit, a cumulative process of expansion sets in.

The argument runs in terms of a theorem. Suppose that the value of wage-goods needed to employ an additional unit of labour in the planned sector is Rs 400 whereas the actual consumption of a corresponding unit in the subsistence sector is Rs 200. Then, if the planned sector can somehow secure an extra saving of Rs 400, the additional employment created will be two units instead of one. For, while with the saving of Rs 400 done in the planned sector one unit of labour is productively employed, the withdrawal of this unit from the subsistence sector is accompanied by a release of Rs 200 worth of wage-goods. This can now be added to another equivalent bundle of wage-goods to be released if one more unit of labour is withdrawn from the subsistence sector. The economy is therefore in a position to absorb altogether two units of labour in productive employment, although the initial dose of saving was just enough for one unit. Saving thus breeds saving, and we have a so-called 'multiplier effect' on employment, the value of the 'multiplier' depending upon the ratio of 'wage unit' in the planned sector to what may be called the 'consumption unit'[2] in the subsistence sector. The lower this ratio, the higher is the value of the 'multiplier'.

## II

So far, so good. The emphasis on the implications of 'disguised unemployment' for the economics of growth is commendable. The proposition that employment is limited by the flow of wage-goods that can be made available to labourers, though apparently commonplace, is worth emphasizing at a time when economic thinking is so widely influenced by the Keynesian theory of effective demand. In an under-developed economy, the scope for expansion of the current output of wage-goods is limited, and the Keynesian investment multiplier is insufficiently operative. Yet an opportunity for a

[1] Vakil and Brahmananda: *Planning for an Expanding Economy* (Bombay, 1956).

[2] The term is used here to signify the actual consumption of a unit of labour.

'cumulative process' offers itself in such an economy if the 'disguised unemployed' is released from the subsistence sector and the 'saving potential' that it carries is used as a supplement to whatever additional savings can be drawn from the rest of the economy. For this to happen, the rate of growth of employment must pass the critical limit set by the growth of population. Our authors' crusade against India's Second Five Year Plan is based largely on this concept. The employment target set in the Plan is much too inadequate to draw in the 'disguised unemployed' and to bring the cumulative process into play.

However, if our authors had reflected upon their hypothesis a little more closely they would perhaps realize that they had started from the wrong end. Not that their proposition is wrong; of course it is not, so far as the arithmetic is concerned. But the way it is presented suggests a certain lack of awareness of the *obstacles* to the growth of an under-developed economy. In their excitement at what they thought was a discovery they forgot to notice that if the proposition were put the other way round, it would take a form which has been familiar to most of us most of the time. Let us revert to our authors' example. The 'consumption unit', as we have called it, is Rs 200 and the 'wage unit' is Rs 400. Assume, with our authors, that along with the transfer of the 'disguised unemployed', the goods that they used to consume in the subsistence sector are also transferred to the planned sector. The market is then provided with an additional Rs 200 worth of wage-goods for each extra unit of labour employed in the planned sector. It is true, then, that if an extra saving of Rs 400 is made available in the planned sector, possibilities will be opened up for the employment of two units of labour instead of one which is the labour content of the extra savings, and the so-called multiplier effect will be operating. Now look at this same thing the other way round. A unit of labour is released from the subsistence sector and with it a bundle of goods worth Rs 200. The consumption unit thus released is not sufficient to provide employment to one additional unit of labour in the planned sector; the market has to somehow secure another Rs 200 worth of wage-goods by way of savings. The transfer of a unit of labour from the subsistence sector releases wage-goods whose value is only one-half of the actual wage that has to be paid if it is to be productively employed. If we look at the matter this way, which is perhaps the more realistic way, the 'consumption-goods multiplier' takes on an altogether different complexion.

One feels tempted, at this stage, to turn back and to see wherein our crucial problems lie. The problem of growth in an under-developed economy with a large and redundant population is basically a problem of capital formation. Employment in the investment goods sector needed for capital formation is no doubt limited at any moment by the availability of wage-goods. But the output of consumption goods in general and of wage-goods in particular is itself a function of the stock of capital. An increase in the stock of capital increases the scope for the employment of labour, although during any given period of investment needed for the production of capital goods, it is the current release of wage-goods that determines the extent to which employment can be increased.

The principal aim of economic planning in an under-developed country is to raise the rate of investment and hence of capital formation with a view to an increasing flow of consumption goods in the future. Since there is a plethora of unemployed in the economy, the speeding up of investment does not require curtailment of activities in the consumption goods sector; the economy can draw upon the reserve of unemployed. If concurrently with the increase of investment there is also increased production of consumption goods, as happens when there is excess capacity in the consumption goods sector, the wage-bill of the additional labourers can be met out of the additional output of consumption goods, and there is no pressure on the consumption goods market. We are, so to say, in the Keynesian world of plenty where an increment of investment leads by itself to an increment of consumption.

It is wrong to suppose that these Keynesian effects are altogether absent in an under-developed country such as India. The capacity in our organized sector does lend itself to fuller utilization, as findings of competent statisticians indicate. Moreover the Plan period that we have in view is not exactly the Keynesian short period where resources and technique are given and fixed; certain investments may well be made to bear fruit during the Plan period. There is, therefore, some scope for the expansion of output of consumption goods to be set against the additional employment in the investment goods sector. But these possibilities are negligible in the context of the volume of investment that is needed to fully absorb the reserve of unemployed, when account is taken not only of the existing volume of 'disguised unemployment' but also of the addition to the labour force resulting from the normal growth of population.

Assume, then, to bring out the essence of the matter, that there is 'full employment' in the organized sector. What happens if, as the need for economic development demands, more employment is to be provided in the investment goods sector towards the production of capital goods? We are in the classical world of Scarcity, and an adequate volume of wage-goods has to be released from the rest of the economy to make provision for the additional labourers engaged in the investment goods sector during the investment period. The rest of the economy has to put up with reduced consumption, the extent of this reduction being determined by the wages-bill (assuming that wages are wholly spent on consumption) of the newly employed labourers. This is the *raison d'être* of 'saving' in the context of the economic development of under-developed countries. It is 'saving' that makes possible an expansion of investment needed for the growth of the economy.

Now, the distinction between 'disguised unemployment' and new labour force generated in the process of population growth is often too sharply drawn. They are not necessarily distinct and separable entities. In practice, very substantially one merges into the other. The major impact of the growth of population in an under-developed economy is on agriculture. And there what happens, as population grows, is that an increasing degree of congestion occurs in the age group that call themselves 'occupied'. The 'saving potential' remains more or less the same, but the mouths to draw upon it increase in number. In fact, the distinction drawn here is not a distinction between two categories of unemployment; it is rather a distinction between two ways of looking at it. However, the distinction becomes analytically significant if we assume that the 'saving potential' gets released for use in the planned sector only at a level of employment beyond what would be needed for the full absorption of the newly emerging labour force. At any rate it is in this sense that the distinction is used here, although it is clear that there is no knowing in practice, at what level of employment this process of release of the 'saving potential' starts operating, if it does operate at all.

Since in the context of the situation that we are contemplating additional employment is devoted entirely to investment and is unaccompanied by any expansion in the output of consumption goods, the wages-bill of the additional labourers has to be matched entirely by 'saving' done in the rest of the economy. In so far as these additional labourers are recruited from the newly emerging labour force, the entire saving needed for meeting their wages-bill has to be newly created. It is only when investment is pushed so far as to enable the economy to encroach on the 'disguised unemployed' that some relief is found, on our assumption, in the release of goods that the labourers drawn into the planned sector used to consume in the subsistence sector. Even here, the 'wage unit' in the planned sector being substantially higher than the 'consumption unit' in the subsistence sector, further new savings have to be created for covering the gap.

## III

All this becomes familiar story, when put in terms of money-wages and prices. An under-developed economy with a reserve of unemployed embarks on a process of planned investment. Additional employment is created in the investment goods sector. Payment is made to the labourers newly employed at the current money rate of wages. These wages are spent on the purchase of wage-goods. There is an increase in the aggregate money demand for wage-goods. If, to start with, there is excess capacity in the consumption goods sector, output of wage-goods expands in response to the increase of demand, and there is no rise of prices, except to the extent warranted by the emergence of bottle-necks here and there. If investment (and employment) is pushed beyond a level where excess capacity is fully exhausted, increased money demand presses on an inelastic supply of wage-goods, and prices start rising. The tendency is checked if the additional expenditure done by the newly employed labourers is offset by reduced expenditure elsewhere in the economy. The need for the offset is only lessened to the extent that there is transfer of wage-goods from the non-monetized sector to the monetized sector where the additional expenditure has its impact. If, therefore, prices of wage-goods are to be held constant in order for the real wage rate not to fall, the volume of additional (planned) savings needed in the monetized sector for the full absorption of the unemployed (disguised and undisguised) would be equal to the total money wages accruing to this entire body of newly employed labourers (assuming that wages are all spent) *minus* the money value at current prices of the increment of output of wage-goods, including the amount transferred from the non-monetized sector.

It is not difficult now to see the kind of hurdles that have to be got over in order for the economy to be able to utilize the 'disguised unemployed' for purposes of development. First, there is the problem, how to create conditions under which the disguised unemployed would get released from the subsistence sector and be drawn into the planned sector? Is wage incentive enough? If not, what 'organizational changes' would be necessary for the purpose? Secondly, supposing that *men* are transferred, what guarantee is there that the *goods* that they were consuming would be transferred, too, to the planned sector? Is it not probable that those who would stay back would choose to retain at least a part of the consumption of the group that are switched on to the planned sector? The exodus of the 'disguised unemployed' will no doubt leave the subsistence sector with a 'surplus' of wage-goods. But those who will be still there will in all probability be reluctant to part with this surplus. This is partly because they will now wish to improve their standard and partly because they will have perhaps some more mouths to feed in view of a possible increase in the number outside the employable age group, as is likely to happen as population grows during the Plan period. What steps could be taken to prevent them from behaving that way? Will the normal price incentive be enough? Above all, thirdly, how are the necessary savings to be created in the economy, so as to cover the gap between the 'wage unit' and the 'consumption unit'? In an economy where normal savings do not take care even of current additions to the labour force, this would appear to be the most serious obstacle to optimum growth, particularly when planning is conceived against the background of a democratic way of life.

5

# CAPITAL AND EMPLOYMENT*

## I

If we can have a process of increasing *per capita* income started somehow, then it is possible to accelerate the process of capital formation by drawing upon a larger and larger proportion of the increment of *per capita* income over time. Suppose, to start with, that the rate of saving is 9 per cent of national income per annum resulting, on the assumption of an output-capital ratio of 1:3, in an increment of national income by 3 per cent per annum. Suppose also that the rate of growth of population is 2 per cent. We have then an increment of *per capita* income by 1 per cent, which is one-third of the rate of increment of aggregate income. We can thus have our people save as much as 33⅓ per cent of the increment of aggregate income over the year and yet maintain the same average level of consumption. This is something which is very significant. Let us look at the figures: 9 per cent is the rate of saving, to start with. If the saving out of the increment of income is also 9 per cent, we have a constant average rate of saving and, on the assumption of a constant output-capital ratio, a constant rate of growth also. On the other hand, if the saving out of the increment of income is more than 9 per cent, the average rate of saving is raised, and there are possibilities of a higher rate of capital formation and a higher rate of growth. We can accelerate the process by saving on the average more and more out of the increment of income till it reaches 33⅓ per cent of the increment of aggregate income. It is only when we go beyond this that the average standard of consumption goes down. There are thus two limits between which the saving out of the increment of income (marginal rate of saving, as we may call it) may be permitted to lie—one set by the original rate which is the minimum needed for preventing a fall in the rate of growth and the other set by the difference between the rate of growth of national income and the rate of growth of population—which is the maximum we can have if the average standard of living is not to fall.

The more we move towards the maximum point the larger will be the income increment itself, out of which we shall be asked to save and the greater therefore will be the possibility of raising the rate of saving and hence the rate of growth. The advantage of having the marginal rate of saving above the average rate is that it has a cumula-

* Originally published in *The Economic Weekly*, Annual Number, January, 1960.

tive effect on the rate of growth, making it rise progressively. And this is what an under-developed economy needs, at any rate over the period unemployment due to capital shortage still remains a problem.

This brings us to a concept which has an important bearing on our present analysis—the concept of labour-capital ratio. Given a certain technology, there is a certain quantity of labour that a piece of capital good can accommodate if worked at full capacity. If we know this relation between each type of capital good and the number of labourers that it can absorb at full capacity, we can work out the average labour-capital ratio for the economy as a whole in the same way as the output-capital ratio is worked out. What the labour-capital ratio tells us, in other words, is the amount of capital in value terms that is used in the economy per person employed. Let us fix upon this concept of labour-capital ratio—$L/C$, where $L$ stands for labour and $C$ stands for capital. This ratio has important bearing on the employment aspect of economic development, even as the output-capital ratio ($O/C$) has on the income aspect. Before we go on to this employment aspect, let us show how the output that we can derive from a unit of labour is given by the ratios that we have already gone into. Let us have a break-down of the ratio of output to labour in the following way:

$$\frac{O}{L} = \frac{O}{C} \div \frac{L}{C}$$

The equation tells us that the output that is associated with a unit of currently employed labour is a function of two ratios—the output-capital ratio and the labour-capital ratio. It rises if the value of $O/C$ rises, $L/C$ remaining the same, and falls if the value of $L/C$ rises, $O/C$ remaining the same. Again—and this is more realistic—it rises if the value of $O/C$ rises more than that of $L/C$ and falls if the value of $L/C$ rises more than that of $O/C$. All this has an important bearing on the choice of technique in economic development. It is sometimes suggested that in an under-developed economy which suffers from shortage of capital, we should adopt techniques which are associated with high output-capital ratio. This seems on the face of it to be unexceptionable. It seems an easy deduction from Harrod's equation $G = S. O/C$, namely that if $S$ (rate of saving) remains constant, then we raise the value of $G$ (growth rate) by raising the value of $O/C$. When one considers this, however, along with the equation set up above, one finds that the deduction is a little too facile. If we can raise the value of $O/C$ through technological and organizational improvements which make capital more efficient, well and good. But if we do it by choosing a technique which is just labour-intensive, i.e. by raising the value of $L/C$, then the procedure becomes dubious.

For while we raise the output per unit of capital, we lower the output per unit of labour.[1]

## II

Now about the employment aspect of economic development. Let us make a few assumptions, to start with. Let us assume that the output-capital ratio (*O/C*), the labour-capital ratio (*L/C*), the rate of population growth, the proportion of labour force to total population are all constant over the period that we have in view. Let us assume further that there is full employment—whatever one means by it—to start with. If then population grows at the rate of 2 per cent per annum, then if full employment is to be maintained over time, aggregate employment must increase at the rate of 2 per cent per annum. Now, since *L/C* is constant, aggregate capital must also increase at the rate of 2 per cent per annum. We shall, therefore, get the same percentage increase in output, assuming what economists call constant returns to scale. For a 2 per cent increase in aggregate output we need a rate of saving of 6 per cent of the national income if, as before, we assume the output-capital ratio to be 1:3.

What does all this mean? It means that under the assumed conditions we have an increase in national income at a constant rate, a constant rate of consumption *per capita* and full employment conditions in the economy over time. I am presenting this simplified picture in order to be able to highlight the complications that beset an under-developed economy of the type that we have in view. Let us remind ourselves of two things which have already been noted, namely that, to start with, we have a large volume of unemployment and average living levels are below standard. So we have two responsibilities. First, we have to raise the rate of employment so as to be able within a prescribed period to absorb the current volume of unemployment; and this will require a rate of investment higher than that postulated above. Further, the more quickly we want to realize a state of full employment, the higher will have to be the rate of investment in the transition period. Suppose, for example, that there is initially a backlog of unemployed of the order of five millions and, considering the rate of population growth and the proportion of labour force to the aggregate population, an addition to the labour force of the order of ten millions over the planning period of, say, five years. Suppose also that in the absence of current unemployment, we would need an investment rate of 6 per cent of annual income for absorbing the yearly additions to the labour force. Then—

[1] One fears that a raising of the value of L/C may be self-frustrating, inasmuch as it may be accompanied by a fall in the value of S and hence of G.

again on the assumption of constant labour-capital ratio—we have to raise the rate of investment to 9 per cent if we wish to attain a level of full employment in the course of five years. If the period of transition is extended we may go in for a lower rate. But in any case the rate has to be higher than 6 per cent.

Secondly, we have to raise the average level of living which, to start with, is below a tolerable minimum. It is true that the productive employment of people who had been hitherto unemployed would in itself mean a rise in *per capita* income. Yet, so long as the output-labour ratio remains the same, the rise in the *per capita* income such as would result from just the absorption of the unemployed cannot be of an appreciable order. After all, the proportion of current unemployment to *total population* cannot be very large in any case; in our economy it will be somewhat around 2 per cent, if we leave out 'disguised' unemployment, and perhaps around 5 per cent, if we include it. If an impression is to be made on *per capita* income, we cannot be content with merely having enough additional capital to provide for the unemployed; we have to raise the output-labour ratio itself.

Now, this latter can be achieved, as we have seen, by raising the output-capital ratio or by lowering the labour-capital ratio. Both involve a change in the technique of production—the former of a capital-saving character, let us say, and the latter of a labour-saving character. In an economy where capital is scarce and labour is abundant, it is clear that capital-saving techniques must be preferred to labour-saving techniques; at any rate the former should be made to overbear the latter. The scope of the former, however, appears to be limited. For, it may well be argued that in so far as there was any such scope, it would be adopted as a matter of course; the scarcity of capital is expected by itself to impose on the economy a full use of any *known* technique of production of the capital-saving variety.

Now of course this is not altogether correct. It so happens that in most of the under-developed economies the price of capital (i.e. the rate of interest) in the organized sector is not as high relatively to the wages of labour as is warranted by the relative degree of scarcity of capital and labour. One does have a feeling that cases can be discovered in the organized sector of our economy of misdirection in the use of capital arising from a divergence between the warranted rate of interest, as we may call it, and the market rate of interest. It is indeed very necessary that in our planned projects—whether in the private sector or in the public sector—calculation of relative costs in respect of different lines of production and in respect of different techniques within each line should be based on an estimate of the warranted rates of interest and wages rather than on the actual rates in the market. Yet when all is said it appears that if we are to have a structure of production which is enough capital-saving to yield a satisfactory output-labour ratio, we must *discover* new lines of production and new techniques. And this involves research and, at the initial stage at any rate, capital to finance research. On the other hand, if new capital-saving devices are not forthcoming, the alternative is to follow the traditional method of industrialization, which is to use techniques involving less labour relative to capital. The latter process is easier, for we can import these techniques already in use in the more developed Western economies. Now this, if widely used, results in what is called technological unemployment. And in order to accommodate this newly created body of unemployed, the economy must be provided with more capital than would be the case if the labour-capital ratio had remained constant. Here again, if, with constant labour-capital ratio, the full employment rate of saving (and investment) is 9 per cent of the national income, as on our previous hypothesis, then it has to be 18 per cent, if the labour-capital ratio is halved, 13·5 per cent if the labour-capital ratio is made two-thirds, and so on. In general terms, if, with a given labour-capital ratio, $L/C$, the full employment rate of saving (and investment) is $S$, then as $L/C$ is changed into $L'/C$, where $L = L'/x$, the new full employment rate of saving (and investment) becomes $Sx$. The extent to which the rate of saving has to be raised under the changed conditions thus depends upon the value of $x$; the higher it is, the higher will be the rate of savings and investment that would satisfy full employment conditions.

The test of economic progress is not just maintenance of full employment. A country which is already advanced and has a high average standard of living can afford to take full employment as a unique goal of economic policy, a certain minimum level of growth being implicit in it. But for an under-developed country such as ours where in the past the rate of capital formation has failed to keep pace with the growth of population and where peoples' standard of living has been systematically pressed down, the essential test of economic progress is rising productivity of labour; maintenance of full employment is not enough. This is what makes the task of economic development of an under-developed economy so formidable. The twin task of creating employment opportunities and raising labour productivity requires the level of saving to be pushed up a good deal higher than the level to which the people are used. In our case, the Planning Commission put the required rate of saving at 17–18 per cent of national income as against the normal level of 5 per cent, as they guess it was at the time planned economic development started. So long as the additional savings are drawn out of annual increments in *per capita* income, the target is obviously within the bounds of possibility. Yet who will deny that the realization of the target involves tremendous organizational effort unlike any that a democratic society has hitherto experienced? It is just this that lends special significance to India's experiment in economic planning.

# 6

# REFLECTIONS ON 'TAKE-OFF'*

## I

It is a property of short, slogan-like expressions that they gain easy currency while remaining undefined or at best imperfectly defined. One uses these expressions without feeling any obligation to explain what it is that they signify. Not having a rigid connotation, they acquire significance by usage. 'Take-off' is one such expression. Borrowing from aeronautic parlance Rostow, an economic historian introduced the term in economic literature to denote a stage in the economic development of a country—a stage which is marked by a process (rapid enough to justify the aeronautic analogy) of change-over from a level of stagnation to what he calls 'self-sustained growth'. And now it is on everybody's lips. Not only growth theorists but also practising planners and even politicians have got into the habit of using the term in the context of economic development of under-developed countries. The term is acquiring special significance in view of the fact that it is believed in many quarters that a number of under-developed countries are currently passing through the so-called 'take-off' stage. It is my belief that the term lacks precision, and yet it is suggestive and can be given an interpretation which is useful for an understanding of the process of economic development of an under-developed country. It is indeed the vagueness of the term that gives it strength, for one can put an interpretation upon it to suit the conditions of the economy in which one is interested. It is the purpose of this paper to attempt such an interpretation in the context of Indian economy.

Obviously, the concept involves three considerations. First, an initial level of the economy which is marked by stagnation. The stagnation may of course refer to the aggregate national income, or it may refer to *per capita* income. The former rules out growth altogether and is characterized by zero net saving and zero net investment. Marx's simple reproduction scheme represents this. The latter, however, is consistent with positive net investment and hence growth, but it rules out more than a minimum investment that maintains a rate of growth of national income which is just equal to the growth of population. There is thus a certain ambiguity here, but this should not cause any trouble. After all the more significant concept in this context is that of *per capita* income, and

* Originally published in *AICC Economic Review*, Bangalore Congress Number, 1960.

whether a stagnant *per capita* income is also accompanied by a stagnant aggregate income or not depends upon whether the economy has a growing population or a stationary population. As economy with a stationary aggregate income cannot surely long maintain a growing population. And since even in a primitive economy, population does grow, our initial level is one where a net investment of some order, however low it may be, does take place.

Secondly, there is the question of the interval. Starting from an initial level of stagnation, what is the period that 'take-off' is supposed to take to reach the final level of 'self-sustained growth'? The expression 'take-off' obviously implies that the period should be short—enough short indeed for the passage to the higher level to show characteristics of an economic revolution. Rostow puts it somewhere between fifteen and twenty-five years, having regard to the growth process of a number of countries which have already reached a higher stage of economic development. The exact period of transition is again not a crucial issue. For whether it marks a 'take-off' or not depends upon the character and magnitude of change that comes over during the period; it is a question of whether the period is capable of being marked off not only from the base which is one of stagnation but also from a final level which is conspicuously higher than the original level and where the economy can be permitted to settle down.

At last we come to the most crucial consideration, namely the character, of the final level. Rostow calls it the stage of 'self-sustained growth'; the stage which the economy is led up to along 'take-off' is a stage of self-sustained growth. Now, what is 'self-sustained growth' and why is the end-point thus described considered to be significant?

There are certain things which are clear and unambiguous. During the low-level stagnation period the production technique in the economy is primitive and there is very little surplus over consumption available for investment for the *per capita* income to rise appreciably. Secondly, during the 'take-off' interval, enough surplus emerges for investment to rise appreciably—a sudden spurt coming either from within or from without, the *per capita* income rises and a regular, yearly rise in the *per capita* income makes it possible for the economy to absorb an increasing proportion of the increment of aggregate income for investment purposes without impairing the average standard of consumption. In technical terminology, the 'take-off' interval is marked by an excess of the 'marginal' rate of saving over the average rate of saving, so that the average rate keeps on rising. Is it, then, that the final level is characterized by a constant, though high, average rate of saving? This does not seem to be a sensible interpretation. For even in a highly developed economy, the average rate of saving may not remain constant. Rostow's dividing line at

10 per cent saving is not convincing either. What is the sanctity about this particular percentage, except that with 10 per cent annual saving, one may expect an economy to acquire a higher trend of *per capita* income unless the capital-output ratio and the rate of population growth are abnormally high. A demarcation along this line is surely arbitrary.

There is a sense of spontaneity in the concept of 'self-sustained growth' which is unmistakable. But here again, unless one is considering a planned economy (where over the initial period of economic development, a special effort is made by the Government Authority to mop up a higher and higher fraction of the annual increments of income and after a level is reached the economy is left to itself to derive sustenance from a spontaneously created surplus), there is hardly any significance in taking the element of spontaneity as a criterion for marking off the stage of 'self-sustained growth'. In the UK or USA even the so-called 'take-off' stage was spontaneous.

## II

The situation, I believe, is less obscure in the context of an economy such as ours, where in the past the growth of population has so far outstripped the rate of economic development that over the years there has emerged an accumulated backlog of unemployment. In such an economy the minimum that the 'take-off' must accomplish is the elimination of this unemployment, besides absorbing in productive employment the additional labour force that emerges as a result of the yearly growth of population. Here the demarcation is clear-cut if, once full employment is secured, the economy is raised to a level where growth is self-sustained and spontaneous. Suppose you have an economy where the over-all capital-output ratio is 3:1 and the rate of population growth is 2 per cent per annum. Suppose also that, production technique being what it is, full employment could be maintained by a rate of investment which is 6 per cent of the annual income. If in such an economy the actual rate of investment warranted by the normal saving rate is less than 6 per cent, you have over the years an accumulation of unemployment. Suppose now, as a result of this process of accumulation of unemployment, the number of unemployed comes up to 5 million at the time you are supposed to start your 'take-off', and suppose further that over the period that you have in view the additional labour force that emerges as a result of the growth of population comes up to another 10 million. Then if you hold the attainment of full employment as the end-point of the 'take-off' process, you have to raise the rate of saving of the community to 9 per cent of the annual income. And this, provided the technique of production in terms of the labour-capital ratio remains the same. But of course, the technique does not remain the same in any process of change-over of an economy to a higher level. Capital is co-operant with labour; it is also its rival. And in the process of industrialization—which is a main feature of the 'take-off' stage, some degree of rivalry between capital and labour must manifest itself. In so far as this happens, the rate of increase of employment turns out to be less than what it would be if the technique of production had remained constant. The 'take-off' stage must, if it is to usher in a progressive economy, be accompanied therefore by a rate of investment which is higher than we have just envisaged. If 9 per cent saving rate ensures full employment on the assumption of constant technique, we require a saving of more than 9 per cent when we allow the technique of production to change in the labour-saving direction. The full employment rate of saving which is, by our definition, the end point of 'take-off' will be the higher, the more the labour-capital ratio is brought down in the process of industrialization; it will be 12 per cent, if the labour-capital ratio is reduced to three-fourths of the initial level 13·5 per cent if the labour-capital ratio is reduced to two-thirds of the initial level; and so on. The twin task of creating employment opportunities and of industrialization of the economy involves a rate of saving which is a good deal higher than the level existing at the time the economy starts the 'take-off', its precise magnitude depending upon the initial volume of unemployment, the growth of labour force consequent on the growth of population and the change in technology that the process of industrialization involves.

In the light of the above, we may perhaps take a look at our Indian economy to see how far along 'take-off' the Plans have carried it. The possible criteria for judging the situation are growth of savings, growth of *per capita* income and the growth of employment and unemployment. Rostow puts India categorically among economies 'attempting "take-off".' The sole test that he applies is that of growth in the rate of savings. Judged by this test surely India is well up on the 'take-off' line; even leaving out foreign aid, the rate of saving and investment in our economy will have gone up under the two Plans presumably from 5 per cent to around 8 per cent of the annual income. Over these years the marginal rate of savings will have been systematically higher than the average rate. The scope of savings has also widened, judged by the rise in the *per capita* income which has gone up by about 18 per cent over the period 1951–9. There is, however, one snag about this latter, arising from the uncertainties that still characterize production in the agricultural sector—witness the fall in the index of *per capita* income from 115·1 in 1956–7 to 111·9 in 1957·8, due obviously to bad harvest. At the physical level also the situation is encouraging if we go by the indices of production of strategic commodities such as iron and steel, cement, electricity etc.

When, however, it comes to employment which is chosen here as the element of overriding importance, the situation is alarming. Judged by the employment criterion, despite all the investment that has taken place over the period, our economy seems to be *receding*. If we started at the time of the formulation of the Second Five Year Plan with an estimate of a backlog of unemployed of the order of 5 million, the corresponding figure on the eve of the Third Five Year Plan is supposed to come up to 7 million. If, therefore, the addition to the labour force consequent on the growth of population over the period of the Third Five Year Plan is going to be of the order of, say, 14 million, as it is expected to be on the assumption of a growth of population of about 2 per cent per annum, then the extra employment for which the Third Five Year Plan must make provision will have to be at least double that which the Second Plan is expected to achieve. It is then that our economy will get on to the 'take-off' stage in any significant sense.

# 7

# APPROACH TO INDIA'S THIRD FIVE YEAR PLAN*

Approach to the Third Five Year Plan is a broad subject, and the contributors have interpreted its scope rather liberally. The topics brought under discussion range from Objectives of Planning to Size and Pattern of Investment, including Finance. Such specific questions as Family Planning. Community Development, Operation of Public Enterprises, etc., have also found a place in some of the papers.

I propose to confine my observations to the following broad items that figure more conspicuously in the papers that fall under this section.

(i) Objectives;
(ii) Size and Pattern of Investment; and
(iii) Organization and Finance.

## I

The broad objectives laid down in the Second Five Year Plan, namely, growth, employment and distributional equity, are generally accepted. The objectives are unexceptionable, and surely they must continue to shape our Plan. It is, however, our business as economists to spell out these objectives a little more clearly and to show the limits of their simultaneous achievement, particularly in the light of our experience of the earlier Plans. Perhaps then we would be led on to consider the organizational changes that would be necessary in this context. We do not live in the Keynesian world where a transfer of income from the rich to the poor increases consumption and hence employment and perhaps also investment—where, therefore, a reduction in the inequality of income may be one of the methods by which employment and growth can be sustained. Ours is an economy where growth is still retarded by shortage of capital resources, where there is still a large backlog of unemployment of a non-Keynesian variety and where the normal saving rate is still less than would permit a rate of investment adequate to absorb the additions to labour force consequent on the growth of population. High rate of growth here implies a high level of investible surplus, and this may

* *Rapporteur's* report to the Indian Economic Conference, 1956, on papers relating to *Approach to the Third Five Year Plan*. Originally published in Indian Economic Association Conference Volume, December, 1959.

involve a technique of production which does not offer a high level of employment. On the other hand, a high level of employment and an egalitarian operation may lead to a level of consumption inconsistent with the maintenance of an investible surplus adequate for our desired growth rate. It must be for our consideration how best we could reconcile these possible conflicts.

Some of the contributors maintain that the Third Plan marks a 'crucial stage' in the process of the economic development of our country. No argument, however, has been advanced to show why this Plan, in particular, should have a special title to being 'crucial'. The idea that some peculiar significance attaches to the Third Plan seems to be based on the perspective indicated in the Second Plan. It may also have something to do with recent discussions concerning the economics of what is often called a 'self-generating' plan. In fact, it is widely held in this country that the next decade should see the economy put firmly along a path of economic development which could sustain itself by its own momentum. It may be recalled that the Second Plan envisaged a raising of the saving rate from 11 per cent to 14 per cent for the Third Plan and from 14 per cent to 17 per cent for the Fourth Plan, and maintaining it thereafter more or less at the same level. The emphasis on heavy industries suggested in the Second Plan also lends support, at the physical level, to the idea of self-generating growth.

The concept of self-generating growth has nowhere been clearly defined, and it is doubtful if a clear-cut definition is at all possible. In a sense any growth system is self-generating in so far as it is characterized by forces operating within the economy which are sufficiently strong to neutralize the depressing effect of population growth and rising marginal propensity to consume, if any. For example—to take a limiting case—if the saving rate is 6 per cent per annum and the capital-output ratio is 3:1, then an investment rate which is equated to the rate of saving will generate a growth rate of 2 per cent per annum, other things remaining the same. Suppose now the growth of population also to be 2 per cent per annum; you have then a constant *per capita* income. If in a system such as this the representative individual's marginal propensity to consume remains constant, too, you have a self-perpetuating growth rate at 2 per cent per annum, with no improvement in living levels.

If, however, the rate of population growth turns out to be at all less than 2 per cent, so that the *per capita* income tends to rise and the individual's marginal propensity to consume tends to fall, you have inherent in your economy forces that make for a progressively increasing rate of growth. In our present context it appears that the significant point is that we create through a high degree of initial effort certain basic conditions in the economy which, considering the resulting increment of *per capita* income and the associated marginal propensity to consume, are calculated to sustain a growth rate in conformity with full employment conditions. In Harrod's terminology this means an effort to reach a stage at which the 'warranted rate of growth' is equated to the 'natural rate of growth', having regard to the fact that the so-called natural rate of growth refers to a point where the backlog of unemployed is already absorbed in the economy. The transition to this final stage must then necessarily be marked not only by an artificially high rate of saving to take care of finance, but also, at the physical level, by an artificially high rate of growth of heavy industries. For, at the final stage and thereafter we must have the required finance automatically generated by way of saving and also the necessary fixed capital to support the system.

This final objective—the end point, as we may call it—of economic planning will perhaps receive general support in the context of an over-populated, under-developed economy such as that of India. On the question, however, as to what should be the duration of the transition, there will surely be difference of opinion, as is evident from the attitude shown in the papers under discussion.

## II

This brings us to the question of size and pattern of investment. The degree of effort we are prepared to put in determines the size and pattern of investment in each phase of planning and this latter in turn determines the duration of transition towards the full employment growth level. The smaller the size of investment and the more quick-yielding its pattern is, the easier is the transition; and *vice-versa*.

How should we choose the size and pattern of investment? The majority of our contributors seem to accept the size envisaged in the Second Plan, viz. Rs 9900 crores, subject to such revisions as are indicated by the rise of prices and the change in the rate of growth of population as revealed since the Second Plan was formulated. A few, however, consider this projection to be a little over-ambitious, having regard to the availability of resources. The pessimism of this latter group apparently arises from the experience of bottle-necks that confronted the Second Plan—bottle-necks relating not only to foreign exchange but also—and perhaps more—to shortage of internal finance.

Surely the experience of the Second Plan fails to inspire optimism. In spite of the very generous foreign assistance that we received during this period—the amount of foreign assistance has indeed exceeded our original estimate—and in spite of a heavy dose of deficit financing, we have had to make a sizeable reduction in our investment target in the public sector. We have had a considerable short-fall on the resources front. Whether, however, this short-fall is due to a basic deficiency in our resources position or it is due to a deficiency in the organization of the system is an open question.

As regards pattern of investment, the majority of the contributors are in favour of the continuance of emphasis on heavy industries, with this reservation that greater attention than was given in the Second Plan has to be devoted to agriculture, if only because of the food shortage that we are currently experiencing. Perhaps also there is a general agreement in favour of a shift from major to minor irrigation and of a general preference for fertilizer as against irrigation in so far as these two are substitutes and not complements. All this suggests an awareness of the need for progress to be tempered by considerations of security. This surely is understandable.

One of the contributors has come out with a suggestion that the phasing of our Plan must be based on the rate of technical progress and the period covered by an agricultural cycle; as such our planning should be for seven years instead of five, as it has been hitherto. It is also suggested in this connexion that there should be a 'minimum variant' and a 'maximum variant' of the Plan, the implementation of one or the other depending upon the degree of favourableness of the situation. This last suggestion may readily be accepted in so far as technically there is scope for flexibility; in fact some allowance for variation of targets is implicit in any Plan. This, however, has little to do with the fixation of the period of planning. One would also find it difficult to see the connexion of the planning period with agricultural cycle or with the rate of technical progress; one should have thought it was essentially a question of how far ahead one could look.

On the whole, one gets the impression from a perusal of the papers that we have our pessimists and our optimists, the former taking their stand on the fact of scarcity, and the latter on the belief that the rigour of scarcity can at least be mitigated by organizational improvements. To this question we may now turn.

## III

No drastic changes in organization have been suggested in any of the papers; there is general appreciation of the urgency to keep within the democratic framework. This certainly is refreshing. In a world where planning has been almost inseparably associated with totalitarianism, no occasion can be missed to stress the need for the preservation of democratic values in our society and to tell people that the path of gradualness is not just a refuge of the coward. While this is true and while it is also true that our Government has unequivocally accepted the democratic path of gradualness in its scheme of planning, it would surely be going too far if one says, as as does one of our contributors, that the role of the State in our planning is for it just to act as 'a countervailing power against monopolistic concentration of economic power'. or that 'the economic philosophy of Indian socialism is a combination of Adam Smith's *Wealth of Nations* and Keynes *General Theory*. Whether the practice of our Government in Socialism is up to its profession or not, it has surely gone beyond Adam Smith and Keynes!

It is interesting that those of our contributors who have a rather pessimistic outlook on the size of the Plan are also in favour of leaving things more to the private sector. While they argue that the plan must be 'realistic' and its size kept within 'available resources', they also favour a reduction in the rate of taxation and giving more encouragement to the private sector. One may well wonder what connexion there is between the two processes. Simply because you want the size of the plan to be moderate, you are not logically compelled to 'mix' the economy with a relatively larger dose of private investment. Nor is there any compelling economic reason why, if the private sector is prepared to accept the challenge, a relatively bigger share of a bigger total of investment should not be assigned to it. It appears on ultimate analysis that these are matters on which one's verdict would depend upon one's attitude of mind. Some are born a little conservative and some are born a little progressive.[1]

The general consensus among our contributors is in favour of greater decentralization of our planning organization. There is indeed a growing awareness in the country that our plan has not been able to rouse as much enthusiasm in our people as one would wish it had. It is widely felt that people's participation in the Plan could be secured only if they were given enough responsibility. The demand expressed in most of the papers for 'planning from below' will, therefore, receive general approval. The introduction of village autonomy through the Panchayat system is a step in this direction.

One may underline in this connexion the proposition suggested in one or two papers that whatever resources can be raised in a particular village unit should be utilized for local development, the idea being that it is then that the village people will take a personal interest in planning and development. One may perhaps take it that

[1]'How Nature does contrive
That every boy and every gal
That's Born into this world alive
Is either a little Liberal
Or else a little Conservative.'

this is already a part of the Planning Commission's thinking. This certainly is a move in the right direction. When linked up with the Community Development and National Extension Service activities this may release forces destined to provide a strong base for economic development in our country. If democratic planning is to be made a success, the starting point has to be the village. The principle of financial autonomy must, however, be read with caution. A general extension of the formula, as done by one of the contributors, suggesting that 'saving generated in one sector should be spent in that sector alone' has an implication which, to say the least, is awkward.

An associated problem is that of the utilization of rural manpower. One should have expected our contributors to devote some attention to this. How is the surplus labour in the rural areas to be gainfully employed? Should our system encourage transfer of surplus labour to the urban sector in so far as resources are available there, or should these resources be dispersed in rural areas to accommodate the surplus labour existing there? The former happens to be the traditional method of industrialization. It is through the proletarianization of rural labour and then absorbing the unemployed in urban areas at depressed wages that industrialization proceeded in most of the economies of the West, planned or unplanned. In over-populated agricultural economies, however, this process raises the question of the creation of enough wages-fund in the urban sector. How could this be done? Is there any mechanism, short of coercion, by which the agricultural surplus created by the transfer of rural labour could be mobilized for use in the urban sector? And if no such mechanism is available, could not the process be reversed? These are questions answers to which can no longer be postponed.

On Finance, there seems to be a fair degree of agreement among the contributors on two things, namely (a) that we should not pitch our reliance on foreign aid too high, if only because of future repayment difficulties, and, (b) that the scope of deficit-financing is much more limited than it was for the Second Plan. Both these are common ground, but their value is just negative. On the positive side, special significance has been given to two sources of finance, namely, (a) profits from public enterprise, and, (b) agricultural taxation. Both these again are in consonance with the recent trend of thinking in the country.

Neglect of agriculture as a source of public revenue in our country has been historical, being bound up with our land revenue system. However, in the context of planning for economic development this largest source of national income cannot surely escape being tapped a little more for the creation of investible surplus. Also pertinent is the emphasis on profits of public enterprises as a source of investment. The debate as to whether public enterprises should be run on profits basis or not is of marginal importance in the context of our economy and perhaps an unnecessary fuss is being made of it in current discussions. They *are* run on profits basis, and as the public sector is expanding rapidly, they are naturally expected to make a significant contribution to the finance of our future plans.

# 8

# INTRODUCTION TO THE THIRD PLAN*

## I

Let us take stock of the achievements and shortcomings of the Second Five Year Plan before we introduce ourselves to the Third Plan. The achievements of the Second Five Year Plan are not inconspicuous, judged by the rate of growth and the increase in the production of strategic commodities. The Plan is expected to end up with an increase in national income of about 20 per cent, a rate higher than that which the economy had achieved during the First Plan. And this in spite of bad harvests during the greater part of the Second Plan period.

The weight of agricultural output in the national economy is so great that even a small shortfall in that sector tends to produce a large effect upon the national output. A growth rate of about 4 per cent per year in the face of three consecutive years of low agricultural output since the Second Plan started is, therefore, no mean achievement.

What is more significant is the rate of expansion of strategic industries. The output of steel increased during the Second Plan by 100 per cent; electricity by 70 per cent; coal by 40 per cent; cement by 90 per cent; and fertilizer by 166 per cent.

The performance in respect of foodgrains has no doubt been the least encouraging. Yet, even here, with all the vicissitudes of circumstances, production has increased by 15 per cent—thus giving the lie to the common apprehension that in its preoccupation with heavy industries the Second Plan neglected agriculture altogether; after all, the growth of food production has exceeded the growth of population, even if slightly.

The rate of growth that the Plan has generated is on the whole satisfactory; it has laid a foundation for an accelerated growth, as seen from the rate of increase of strategic commodities like iron and steel, cement, fertilizers, etc. And yet in some sense the Plan has failed. It has failed to achieve many of the targets that had been set originally, and in certain directions the shortfall has been serious indeed.

In most of the strategic commodities the achievement has been

* Originally published in *Seminar* (Delhi), September, 1960.

below the target. In iron and steel the shortfall is 42 per cent, in electricity it is 16 per cent, in cement 32 per cent, in coal 12 per cent and in fertilizer 27 per cent of the respective targets. Only in machine tools among strategic commodities, has the achievement gone beyond the target.

Foodgrains production, again contrary to the common belief, has been on a par with the original target, even though it is a little below the revised target. The over-all position is also below what had been originally envisaged for the Second Plan; the increase in national income over the Plan period is anticipated to be at least 5 per cent below the target.

Secondly, although the over-all investment in the Second Plan will turn out to be very near the target of Rs 6200 crores (at 1952–3 prices), the distribution between the public sector and private sector will be substantially different from what was originally contemplated. The ratio originally contemplated was 60:40; recent estimates suggest it to be in the neighbourhood of 50:50—the private sector having had a more generous deal.

Thirdly, whereas the target for savings, as originally contemplated, was of the order of 11 per cent of the national income, recent estimates place the ratio at 8 per cent. This surely is a serious shortfall, indicating a vital deficiency in our planning. If the over-all investment was kept up, it was because of larger foreign assistance and larger drafts on sterling balances than were originally envisaged.

Finally, on the employment front, the target was to take on an additional 10 million, while recent estimates suggest that the plan will end up with an additional employment of just about 8 million. There will thus be an addition of about 2 million to the backlog of 5 million with which the Plan had started. This also is a vital crack in our plan edifice. What kind of a plan is it, one will surely ask, if it leads up to as much as a 40 per cent increase in the volume of unemployment in five years, whereas the growth of population during the period is only about 11–12 per cent?

## II

According to whether one turns one's eyes on the deficiencies or the achievements of the Second Five Year Plan one tends to become a pessimist or an optimist in one's conception of the Third Plan. And this is what has happened here. We have our pessimists and our optimists—one group contending that the Third Plan must be a moderate plan set by the limits of finance which, on the domestic front, has been found to be discouraging, the other pleading for a bold plan so framed as to take full advantage of the achievements of the Second Plan.

Indeed, recent controversy has related more to size than any other aspect of the Plan. The objectives enunciated in the Second Plan still continue to guide our thinking; indeed they are unexceptionable. There is not much scope for difference on the question of investment pattern either; such difference as has often been exhibited is rather of marginal importance.

A little more emphasis on agriculture than was given in the Second Plan, if only because of food shortage; perhaps a little shift away from major to minor irrigation and from irrigation over to fertilizer in so far as these two are substitutes; a little more care for the 'social services'; these are about all the adjustments that the critics of the Second Plan asked for. The emphasis on a policy of industrialization with a special accent on heavy industries still continues to dominate our thinking.

Even on the mode of finance, there is more or less general agreement to the effect that taxation and profits from public enterprise must play a relatively larger part than they did in the Second Plan and, further, that the scope of deficit-financing is very much less now than it was when the Second Plan was formulated. A fair degree of agreement on this latter point seems to be one of the more refreshing features of our thinking on the Third Plan.

Even the most unorthodox among us would perhaps agree that the limit to deficit-financing in the Third Plan must be set by just one consideration—the rate of growth of consumption goods during the period of the Plan. The extra cushion that the economy had at the commencement of the Second Plan to absorb the impact of deficit-financing is no longer there; for one thing, the sterling balances have been practically exhausted and, for another, the Third Plan takes its start from a base where the price level is already about 20 per cent higher than the base where the Second Plan started from, whereas the latter had a base which was about 15 per cent *below* the First Plan base.

In all these matters the draft outline of the Third Five Year Plan, just presented to the public by the Planning Commission, reflects ideas which are generally accepted. Agriculture, industry and power have received somewhat greater emphasis in the Third Plan than they did in the Second. The outlay ratio has been raised from 6·9 to 8·6 per cent in agriculture; from 19·1 to 20·7 per cent in industry and minerals, and from 8·9 to 12·8 per cent in power. There has been also a shift away from major and medium irrigation, the outlay ratio on this item being cut down from 9·8 to 9·0 per cent.

A little disappointment may perhaps be felt in certain quarters at the reduction in the outlay ratio in respect of 'social services' from 18·7 to 17·2 per cent. But after all if you want to raise the ratio at some point you have to lower it elsewhere. And if proper emphasis is maintained at strategic points within 'social services', a little reduction in the over-all ratio is in order.

The mode of financing the Plan indicated in the draft outline will surely please the more orthodox among our economists. And indeed, given the size of the Plan, the relative emphasis given to the different sources of finance is just what the circumstances would dictate. Rightly has deficit-financing been assigned a much less important role in the financing of the Third Plan.

A few will think, however, that the pendulum has swung the other way—whereas in the Second Plan the ratio of deficit-financing to total Plan outlay in the public sector was more than 25 per cent, in the Third Plan it is proposed to be just about 8 per cent. Indeed, if the food target of 100–5 million tons (registering about a 40 per cent increase over the 1960–1 level) is realized, then it is most unlikely that the additional money demand which would be generated in the economy, given the proposed order of investment and of deficit-financing, will be sufficient to carry off the supply at current prices. If the operation of the Second Plan has pushed up food prices, the operation of the Third Plan—in case the various sectors behave as contemplated—will perhaps pull them down.

Those who regard stabilization of food prices as the core of price policy would certainly favour a raising of the level of deficit-financing. Even then in the present circumstances the safe limit to deficit-financing would perhaps be of the order of Rs 700 crores—i.e. to say, about 10 per cent of the Plan outlay in the public sector.

## III

The really controversial aspect of the Third Five Year Plan is its size. The draft outline places the total Plan investment at Rs 10,200 crores (at 1958–9 prices), of which Rs 6200 crores will be in the public sector and Rs 4000 crores will be in the private sector. The distribution may appear to some to be a little too generous towards the private sector, considering the fact that the goal of Indian economic policy is still recognized to be the establishment of a socialist State. But the issue is not crucial in the present context; after all even as it is, the ratio does mark an advance over the Second Plan as it has turned out to be. The crucial issue is not so much the division of the cake as the cake itself.

The determination of the size of investment for a plan may rest on a number of considerations. One may relate it to an income target or an employment target; one may also derive it from the achievement of past plans, or from the rate of progress realized in other economies in similar circumstances. In any case, some kind of a target is to be kept in view with reference to which resources—

financial and physical—are mobilized. It is a wrong procedure in planning to start from the availability of finance, if only because it may degenerate into acceptance of a line of least resistance.

One is reminded here of the textbook distinction between private finance and public finance to the effect that whereas in the former, expenditure is adjusted to income, in the latter, income is adjusted to expenditure. Planning is, if anything, an extension of the area of public finance. And there is no reason why the principle of public finance should not apply to planning. In planning, as much as in public finance, expenditure—which in the context of development is what we call investment—has a prior claim for consideration, to be fixed with reference to some sort of a target; resources are then to be adjusted to it, even though the determination of the target itself may have to be based on an estimate of the range of possibilities of resource mobilization.

The rate of growth envisaged for the Third Five Year Plan in the draft outline is an increase of national income by 25 per cent over the five-year period. This is a reasonable expectation when it is remembered that the investment ratio contemplated is about 14 per cent of the national income at the end of the Plan. Yet it is certainly a conservative target.

Countries like China, Yugoslavia, Japan and West Germany have, under different systems of economic organization and in varying circumstances, shown much higher rates of growth—in some cases the growth rate exceeding 10 per cent per annum. Even when account is taken of the fact that conditions in India are, on social and institutional grounds, less favourable to growth, the fact remains that a growth rate of less than 5 per cent per annum cannot, by modern standards at any rate, be said to indicate 'rapid economic development'. The deficiency stands out more sharply when it is remembered that out of an investment of Rs 10,200 crores about Rs 2200 is to be financed by 'budgetory receipts corresponding to external assistance'.

While the growth rate envisaged for the Plan may not be inspiring, it is not depressing either. For, with an income growth of about 5 per cent per year and a population growth of a little over 2 per cent per year, we shall have a rise in *per capita* income of about 3 per cent per year, which, compared to our past achievements, is a move forward.

The position, however, becomes different when the size of investment is considered in relation to the employment needs of the economy. Here the picture that comes out is disconcerting. The Planning Commission expects that the proposed volume of investment will secure employment for 14 million persons—10·5 million outside agriculture and 3·5 million in agriculture.

Now, this seems to be rather a pious wish. Our past experience of the operation of the Second Plan shows that an investment of the order of Rs 6750 crores could provide employment altogether to 8 million persons—6·5 million outside agriculture and 1·5 million in agriculture. This gives an investment-labour ratio of about Rs 8440. On this basis, the employment possibility arising out of an investment of Rs 10,200 crores works out to only about 12 million persons. This means that while the Third Plan starts with a backlog of about 7 million unemployed, it ends up with an unemployment figure of 10 million—3 million out of a total of 15 million of new entrants being added to the current backlog. This surely is more than the economy should be asked to bear.

Will, then, the pattern of investment in the Third Plan be made more labour-intensive than it was in the Second Plan? Unless a more minute breakdown of the lines of investment is shown and the labour coefficients of individual pieces of investment are worked out, one cannot be sure as to what precisely is aimed at. The broad distribution of Plan outlay shown in the draft outline does not seem to suggest any significant deviation from the Second Plan pattern.

However, even if the investment-labour ratio is brought down by varying the pattern of investment, the implication of the procedure for the productivity of labour must not be lost sight of. When investment increases by 50 per cent and employment associated with it is made to increase by 75 per cent—for this is what the Plan is supposed to aim at—it is almost inevitable that labour productivity should fall in the course of the operation of the Plan. And if it does, the prospect surely is disconcerting.

The need for an upward revision of the investment target follows inevitably from our analysis. The minimum that one would suggest is an order of investment that would provide employment to 14 million persons consistently with the maintenance intact of the productivity of labour.

The question is still open, and the attitude of the Planning Commission in this respect, as in so many others, is anything but inflexible. The caution which characterizes the Commission's approach to the question stems, it appears, from an over-much pre-occupation with 'finance', to the neglect of 'resources' as such.

In the food target, for example, there is a potential for an expansion of the economy which does not seem to have received sufficient appreciation. In case the target is realized—and of course its realization is not outside the bounds of possibility—we shall have about 40 per cent increase in food production over the 1960–1 level. This should, with a proper organizational support, make possible a larger investment than is assumed in the draft outline. At any rate the matter deserves reconsideration.

# 9

# A PLEA FOR A BOLDER PLAN*

## I

The economist has a tendency to turn a pessimist. A certain degree of pessimism is imposed upon him by the fact that he takes 'scarcity' as the basis of his science. If resources are scarce, obviously there is a certain natural limit to the progress of an economy. So much has been the preoccupation of some of our economists with the concept of 'scarcity' that they would go to the length of suggesting that the only problem that comes within the province of economic science is the problem of allocation of resources; the *volume* of resources under employment has to be taken as part of given 'data'. That the economic problem transcends inter-industry allocation and covers inter-temporal allocation, too, is often forgotten.

Excessive preoccupation with price analysis within a static framework which has been the characteristic of the development of economic science during the period between Marx and Keynes is largely responsible for this. The attitude should have changed in the post-war period, thanks to the advent of the idea of planning and the revival of interest among economists in the theory of growth. A planner cannot obviously tie himself down to a rigid notion of scarcity; his whole approach is based on the principle that inter-temporal allocation of resources as much as inter-industry allocation is capable of being controlled. And once the economist accepts this hypothesis he also accepts the principle that productive resources are, at any rate within limits, elastic and capable of being used in ways which accelerate the growth of an economy. Consume a little less and invest a little more out of your income, and you have an enhancement of your capital resources. Once the initial push is given, the process of expansion of resources gathers momentum; for in growth itself there is inherent a potential for saving. As income increases over time, there is possibility of a larger share of the increment of income being devoted to investment, thus opening the way to a progressive accumulation of capital and a progressive strengthening of the base for economic growth. This indeed is the principle underlying the concept of planning for the economic development of under-developed countries.

We in India have had ten years of economic planning leading, according to the estimates of the Planning Commission, to an increase of national income (at constant prices) by about 42 per cent,

* Originally published in *AICC Economic Review*, Vol. XII, No. 7, 1960.

of *per capita* income by about 20 per cent and *per capita* consumption by about 16 per cent. By modern standards these certainly will not be regarded as spectacular achievements. Yet they are not mean achievements either, considering the economic stupor the economy had been in for years before planning started. It is true that a large part of these achievements is due to foreign assistance and drafts on previously accumulated sterling balances, the contribution of current domestic savings being rather low. Yet, when the initial hurdle is over and the economy has been set along an upward-sloping path, our planners should have exhibited more confidence than they have done in their *Draft Outline* for the Third Five Year Plan.

The approach to the Third Five Year Plan, as shown in the *Draft Outline*, is timid, when account is taken of the legitimate aspirations of our people. The size of investment contemplated is of the order of Rs 10,200 crores—just about 50 per cent higher than the investment realized in the Second Plan, whereas the latter was about double the investment that had been made in the First Plan. This is contrary to what one would expect, considering the fact that we are just entering the 'crucial' stage of our planning. The growth rate contemplated is just about 5 per cent per year as against a rate of about 4 per cent that the Second Plan actually achieved against all odds—partly natural and partly organizational. The income target looks particularly uninspiring when compared with the achievements of other countries where special efforts at economic development have been made in the post-war period. The average growth rate over the period 1952–8 in China, for example, has been 7·6 per cent, in Western Germany 9·54 per cent, in Japan 10·4 per cent and in Yugoslavia about 17 per cent—this last country having recorded a spectacular progress. These countries have achieved what progress they have made under different systems of economic organization and in varying circumstances. Conditions in India are supposed, on social and institutional grounds, to be less favourable to growth. And yet, even in the Indian context, a growth rate of 25 per cent in five years, as envisaged in the Third Plan, would not appear to be at all impressive—particularly when one remembers that our long-term target, as shown in the Second Plan projection, was, with base 1950–1, to double the national income by 1966–7 and the *per capita* income by 1973–4, and further when account is taken of the fact that in the operation of the Second Plan itself we have lost some ground already.

## II

It may be argued that there is nothing sacrosanct about the model projection given in the Second Five Year Plan and that the ground lost is irrevocable. It may also be argued that public response to planning in our country has been low, as indicated by the slow rate of increase in domestic savings—since the beginning of the First Plan our domestic saving ratio is estimated to have increased from 5 per cent of our national income to just about 8 per cent. In the absence of external support, this would hardly make for a growth rate of 3 per cent. This, however, points only to our organizational limitation, and is proof that enough effort was not put in for the mobilization of resources; there was nothing inherent in the growth rate itself which would make for such low domestic savings ratio.

The deficiency in the size of the Third Plan comes out more conspicuously when one turns to employment prospects. This is a point which needs underlining. Unemployment is a drag on an economy; it is a social nuisance and a source of political trouble. But above anything it is a conspicuous waste, worse in its effect on the economy than unused land or unused capital equipment. A day's labour lost is a permanent loss, the 'non-user cost' (as we may call it, adapting a terminology of Keynes) being the entire potential product of labour, whereas in the case of land it is nil (probably negative sometimes, for a piece of land kept fallow for a time assumes higher fertility) and in the case of capital equipment it is negligible, when a long view is taken.

Judged by the criterion of employment the achievement of the Second Plan is particularly depressing, and the prospects of the Third Five Year Plan do not look better if we adhere to the investment figure suggested in the Draft Outline. The Planning Commission expects that an aggregate investment of Rs 10,200 crores will provide employment opportunities for 14 million persons—3·5 million within agriculture and 10·5 million outside agriculture. If the expectations are realizable, consistently with the maintenance intact of the productivity of labour, well and good. The target of 14 million proposed by the Planning Commission does seem to accord with an important criterion, namely that it keeps the proportion of outstanding unemployment to total population constant over time. And this surely is the minimum one would ask for. One fears, however, that the proposed investment will fail to realize even this target. On a broad view of the matter, it appears that the proposed investment of Rs 10,200 crores will provide employment at best for 12 million persons—about 2 million within agriculture and about 10 million outside agriculture. This is on the assumption that the over-all investment-labour ratio remains more or less the same as it was in the Second Plan. On the other hand, if the pattern of investment in the Third Plan is adjusted in such a way as to realize the employment target of 14 million, then, unless drastic organizational improvements are effected, the productivity of labour will come down. And this latter contingency is contrary to the basic idea of economic progress.

Could, however, the organization of the productive apparatus be improved to an extent that would be needed to maintain the productivity of labour on a lower investment-labour ratio? One cannot say; the effectiveness of organizational changes is uncertain. If, indeed, the economist talks more of investment and less of organization in the context of planning, it is because the effect of investment on output, given other things, can be worked out more or less precisely, while the effect of organization cannot be. Further, whatever effects organizational changes may produce on labour efficiency, they assert themselves slowly. It is extremely unlikely, therefore, that these effects would be strong enough over a five-year period to overbear the depressing effect on labour productivity of a reduction in the investment-labour ratio.

The way out is to increase the size of investment. On the assumption of the same investment-labour ratio that, according to the estimates of the Planning Commission, we had in the Second Five Year Plan, the aggregate investment that is called for in the Third Plan is about Rs 11,800 crores at 1958–9 prices. Translated in terms of 1952–3 prices on which the model projection in the Second Plan was made, it comes to just about Rs 10,450 crores. This, let us recall, is only Rs 550 crores higher than the investment figure shown for the Third Plan in the model projection.

Is this attainable? There is nothing inherently impossible about it. As it is, the Planning Commission seems to be satisfied with a marginal investment ratio of 20 per cent; only one-fifth of the increment of income during the Plan period is proposed to be put in as investment. If the various sectors behave in the way suggested in the *Draft Outline*, then the economy is expected to have an annual increase in the output of consumption goods by 3·75 per cent. If now the growth of population is at an annual rate of 2 per cent, our people will still have an improvement in their consumption level on the average at an annual rate of 1·75 per cent. This surely is not 'conspicuous austerity', considering the exigencies of circumstances. If, then, the marginal investment ratio is raised from 20 per cent to, say, 33⅓ per cent, or, in other words, if one-third of the increment of income is drawn out for investment, the size of investment will increase while the people will still enjoy the benefit of a higher standard of consumption. What is more—with an increase in the size of investment there will be a corresponding increase in the growth rate itself, thus supplying a flow of income out of which additional investment resources could be drawn. It is from recognition of this two-way relation between investment and output that a planner derives his confidence and optimism.

# 10

# THOUGHTS ON PUBLIC FINANCE*

## I

A friend of mine once asked me this question: why do we have to pay a part of our income every month to the State? And why, if we are in any case left with a smaller income than is shown in office accounts, should not the salary itself be fixed at a lower level? What —and this was my friend's dilemma—is the fun in our signing a book which shows a salary higher than what we actually receive at the end of the month? The question seemed a naïve one—it was indeed naïve—yet in answering it, I remember, I had to cover a whole gamut of problems connected with public finance. For the purpose of taxation, in the broad sense, is coterminous with the finance of a government.

If the government of a country has to operate as an agency charged with certain functions involving expenditure, it has to have command over a part of the real income of the country. The functions of the government may consist in the maintenance of law and order, security and defence; they may also extend to other spheres, social and economic, depending upon the degree of State interventionism that the society is prepared to accept. Maintenance of internal order and protection against external aggression are of course the minimal function of the State. But no civilized government can stop at this; health and education and certain essential amenities to those sectors of a society which cannot by themselves make provision for these are also part of the responsibilities of a civilized State. In the purely economic sphere, too, awareness is being increasingly felt nowadays of the need for the State to step in to supplement private enterprise not merely to cover up excess capacity where it exists, as in a mature economy, but also to create additional capacity where it is needed, as in an under-developed economy.

To perform its various functions the State needs goods and services which have to be paid for. To have command over a part of the real income of the society, the State needs to appropriate a corresponding part of the money income. And since it is the sum total of the money incomes of individuals that constitutes the aggregate money income of the society, the State has necessarily to encroach upon individuals' money incomes, in so far as such encroachment is deemed appropriate. In a totalitarian society, where

* Originally published in *Seminar*, March, 1963.

production is more or less centralized, it is possible for the State to appropriate the resources which it needs straightaway *before* incomes reach the hands of individuals. But in a predominantly free enterprise economy, it is after incomes reach their destination through a certain process of distribution that the State comes forward to snatch away a portion, either in a direct way via income tax or in an indirect way via commodity tax.

The crucial point in any case is that the entire money income of the society cannot be left at the disposal of the so-called income earners; a part has to be given over to the State for it to dispose of it in a manner dictated by the functions that it assumes. This is irrespective of the level of money income of the society. If all of us were wage-earners and if all production were in the hands of the private sector, then a general cut of 10 per cent of our wages would only mean, the real income of the society in terms of physical output remaining the same, a fall in the general price level; it is this reduced money income that would now purchase the whole of the output.

If, on the other hand, the wage-earners were asked to pay out to the State 10 per cent of their wages in the form of tax, and if the tax receipts of the State were also spent on the purchase of goods, then the wage earners would be denied 10 per cent of the output of the society; their disposable income would be lower than their so-called earned income by 10 per cent, the balance being transferred to the State. A tax on money income deprives the income earners of a part of the real income of the society and enables the State to have command over it; a general cut in money income does not. This, in a nutshell and abstracting from complications arising out of the mixed character of most economies, is the answer to the question with which we started.

But then there is an alternative way in which the State can get round this straight method of taxation—it can sell securities and thereby obtain funds. When these securities are sold to individuals and held by them, the loans behave in a manner similar to a tax so far as their impact upon the economy is concerned; they result in a transfer of income to the State. When the securities are sold to the Central Bank, new money is created with which the State can surreptitiously in a way, take away a part of the real output of the society. An intermediate case is one in which the securities are sold in the first instance in the market, but they are made negotiable and are permitted to pass on to the Central Bank via the general banking system. In either case the State receipts are an addition to the money income that is generated in the normal course of production.

## II

When, about forty years ago, I was a student in the university, we used to be taught that any expenditure of the State in excess of current revenue was to be shown in the budget as a deficit and that budget deficits were injurious to the health of the economy and must be shunned as far as possible. According to this philosophy, tax revenue should be the only source of State expenditure barring that part of it which is covered by fees for specific services whose beneficiaries can be identified and prices of products of State undertakings, such as public utilities. Now, in so far as State economy is treated as an independent entity, divorced from the general economy of the society, this would appear to be a sound philosophy. Living beyond means is surely bad economy, and when the practice is pursued by a body like the State which is privileged, thanks to its own laws regulating note issue, to get on with it with impunity, it may turn out to be dangerous economy. No wonder, therefore, that economists used to look with disfavour upon any tendency on the part of the State to continue with budget deficits for any length of time. Over a short period of depression there might be a fall of revenue and a deficit might occur, but such deficit must be covered, they would argue, by a surplus realized during the boom which would follow it. Long-term balancing of the budget used to be a generally accepted tenet of public financing.

There were, however, two exceptions. First, sale of securities would be permitted in those cases where the expenditure was of a 'productive' character and where the net product of the capital employed would at least cover the interest on the corresponding loan. This again was a sound business proposition applied to State financing. Secondly—and this sounds surprising even today when our thoughts have deviated so much from old orthodoxies—a distinction would be drawn between 'ordinary' expenditure and 'extraordinary' expenditure (I almost hear my old professor's accent on 'ordinary' and 'extraordinary'!), and resort to loans would generally be conceded in the case of the latter. War expenditure, which of course is extraordinary, would thus be permitted to be covered by loans, usually with the reservation that new taxation should be imposed simultaneously to an extent which was at least sufficient to provide the interest on these loans.

Now, the concept of public finance has shifted in recent years, following an enlargement of the concept of the responsibilities of the State. We have learnt to recognize State finance as an integral part of the general economy of the society. We now know that, where an economy suffers from chronic under-utilization of resources, budget deficits are to be not merely tolerated but justified as means of filling in the utilization gap, whether or not the particular enterprise which the State takes up is by itself productive enough to pay for the interest on loans. In the context of economic development, too, similar deficits are generally sanctioned, in so far as the expansion of money resulting from them is not out of proportion with the growth of national output during a given period.

In our own country, for example, we have gone to the length of shedding the old concept of budget deficit altogether and reckoning only that part of our public expenditure as constituting deficit which is financed by the sale of treasury bills to the Reserve Bank. This extreme procedure may or may not be valid on strictly scientific grounds. But it does indicate the distance which we have travelled away from the old rules of public finance, not only in practice but also in theory.

Yet even today, in spite of the liberalization of our ideas on deficit-financing, one would find it difficult to see how there could be any sanction, on economic grounds, for financing war (or, shall we say, defence) expenditure by loans. One must not miss the vital difference between public expenditure for economic development or for maintaining full employment, and public expenditure for building up army and defence equipment. One is productive; the other is not. One carries with it a process of expansion of output; the other does not have any such implication. And in so far as loans through sale of government securities tend, directly or indirectly, towards an expansion of money, they have little justification, on strictly economic grounds, in the context of war expenditure which does not add to the nation's output in any tangible way.

## III

The objectives of taxation are thus about coterminous with the functions of the State. All ordinary expenditure of the State, such as is needed for the maintenance of law and order, defence etc., must be covered by tax revenue. Where the economy suffers from under-utilization of resources, deficit-financing is no doubt indicated to an extent necessary for filling in the utilization gap. There is also a case for deficit-financing, if kept within limits so as not to engender a price rise, when the State takes upon itself the responsibility of planning economic development through public investment of a productive character.

But we would be deceiving ourselves if we thought that war expenditure or large defence expenditure of the sort that India, for instance, is confronted with at the moment in view of the Chinese aggression, just because it is extraordinary, could also be left to be covered by deficit. Since these expenditures are large and since there is a certain psychological resistance on the part of the taxpayers to high rates, a government may often be forced to resort to the loan method or to direct inflation in the context of war finance. But this must not lead one into thinking that the procedure is economically sound.

The loan method may no doubt turn out to be a success, provided it is operated in such a way that it does not lead to a rise of prices. But, in so far as this happens, loans are seen to behave like taxes, being a mere transfer from individuals to the State; their impact upon the society—distribution of income apart—turns out to be the same as it would be under a system of taxation. In fact, it is possible to conceive of a system of compulsory loans to meet these expenditures which would just be a substitute of a system of taxation both from the point of view of the aggregate transfer and from the point of view of the personal distribution of income. But if that is so, why throw people off the scent by having a round-about system instead of a straight one of taxation? If a system of compulsory loans is called for in such emergencies, it should rather be confined to those whose incomes are below the tax exemption limit; for the system would carry with it a built-in process of redistribution of income in favour of the relatively poor, the rich having to bear the burden of interest payment after the period of emergency will be over.[1]

This at last brings us to the question of distribution of income and the role of taxation in mitigating inequality. It is generally agreed that gross inequalities are bad and that it is one of the responsibilities of the State to see that inequalities of income are reduced as far as possible without injuring national output. In fact, moral considerations apart, continuance of large inequalities is detrimental to the stability of a society, and if maintenance of social stability is recognized to be a function of the State, measures are called for which would lead to a transfer of income from the rich to the poor. Taxes and subsidies are a means of achieving this.

Even if other functions of the State were left out, a good case could be made out for a policy of taxation just for the sake of effecting such transfers. The State might step in to collect a part of the income of the relatively rich and spend it towards the provision of social amenities to the poor. Such operations indeed are a common feature of the activities of a modern State. In the discharge of its general functions, too, the State has to recognize this social responsibility. And this it does by distributing the burden of taxation in such a way that it falls more on those who are richer than on those who are poorer. The principle of progressive taxation rests on this.

[1] See my paper on Defence Finance: 'Compulsory Savings for the Poor', *The Economic Weekly*, January 19, 1963.

In an economy where resources remain idle because of a tendency on the part of the rich to save too much, this redistribution through taxes and subsidies may, by raising the aggregate level of consumption, result in larger employment and output. Even where the problem of excess capacity does not exist, redistributive measures, if kept within proper limits, may energize the beneficiaries to an extent which would outweigh the dampening effect, if any, produced elsewhere. This is an aspect of the matter which has to be borne in mind particularly in emergencies such as wars. Measures which are regarded as too bold in the tranquil state of a society may find ready acceptance in a state of emergency.

Having this in mind, one would indeed feel sympathy with a proposal which has come from some of our economists, namely, that to meet the present emergency in our country, progression in taxation should be carried to the extent of fixing a ceiling on individual incomes. A 100 per cent tax on slabs above a certain level of income deemed permissible in the present state of our economy is surely an understandable proposition.

# *Part II*

# RELATIVE PRICES

# 11

# THE USE OF CURVES IN THE ANALYSIS OF MARKET PRICE*

## I

There is a striking passage in Marshall's famous article on Distribution and Exchange: 'The fact is, that twenty years ago I abandoned the use of curves for market problems because they were not really wanted; and I found people would not heed the note of warning that the curves for the normal problem relate to *rates of production and consumption* and those for market curves (*sic*) to *amounts bought and sold*.'[1] Marshall reiterates it in one of his letters to Edgeworth: 'You know I never apply curves or mathematics to market values. I found that, if I once got people to use Demand and Supply curves which discussed *stocks* along the axis of *x*, they could not easily be kept from introducing the notion of stock when flow was essential.'[2] The object of this paper is to examine the implication of this note of warning.

Let us see what the curves usually employed for the purpose teach us. The problem, let us remind ourselves, relates to the formation of price in a daily market. Two persons (or two groups of persons), *A* and *B*, have in their possession fixed stocks of two goods *X* and *Y* respectively, and they come to the market to interchange them. The dealers have their individual preference systems regarding the two goods, which can be shown in terms of indifference curves. From these indifference curves we can also derive their respective offer curves. What light do these curves throw on the determination of the equilibrium of exchange? Do they tell us what price ratio would evolve as a result of the higgling and bargaining of the two parties and what amounts of the goods would be interchanged? Let us have a look into the relevant diagrams.[3]

A given stock *OX* of *X*, measured along the horizontal axis, is held by *A*; and a given stock *OY*, measured along the vertical axis,

* Originally published in *The Indian Economic Journal*, July, 1954.

[1] *The Economic Journal*, Vol. VIII, p. 46. Italics mine.

[2] *Memorials of Alfred Marshall*, ed. Pigou, (London, 1925), p. 435.

[3] The origin of the curves used here can be traced to Edgeworth's *Mathematical Psychics* (Part I, section on Economical Calculus). But a succinct account of the various implications of the curves is given by Bowley in Chapter I of his *Mathematical Groundwork of Economics* (Oxford, 1924), from where the diagrams used in the text are adapted.

is held by $B$. The indifference curves $I_0$, $I_1$, $I_2$ etc., of $A$ are superimposed upon the indifference curves $i_0$, $i_1$, $i_2$ etc., of $B$ with reference to the same origin $O$; and their offer curves $OA$ and $OB$ are placed alongside of one another, so that they intersect at $P$. $CC_1$, called the *contract curve*, is the locus of points of tangency between $A$'s indifference curves and $B$'s indifference curves; the intersection of the offer curves, also a point where a pair of the indifference curves

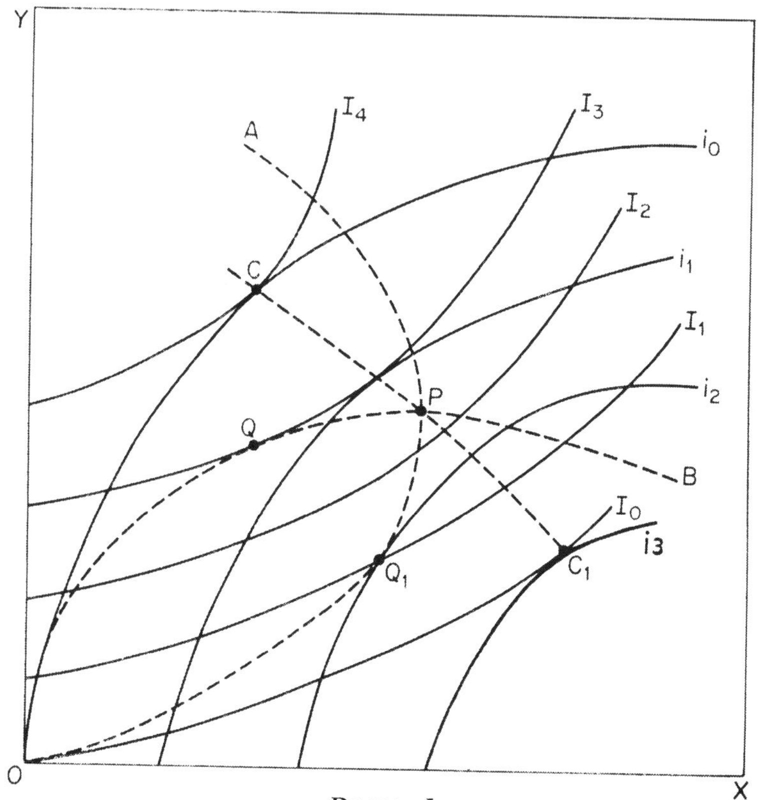


DIAGRAM I

touch one another, thus lies on the contract curve. $Q$ is the point of tangency between $B$'s offer curve and one of the indifference curves of $A$, and $Q_1$, is the point of tangency between $A$'s offer curve and one of the indifference curves of $B$. All this is shown on Diagram I. Diagram II just takes over the section relating to the offer curves.

## II

The following conclusions emerge from these constructions:

(a) If the transactions proceed by trial and error—if, that is to say, the equilibrium process consists of successive bargains at rates of interchange which are revised after each transaction, the final equilibrium will lie somewhere on the contract curve. With the completion of each transaction $O$ will vary and there will be a revision of the rate of interchange. The market will close with a rate which will be given by the common tangent to a pair of indifference curves; for, outside it neither of the

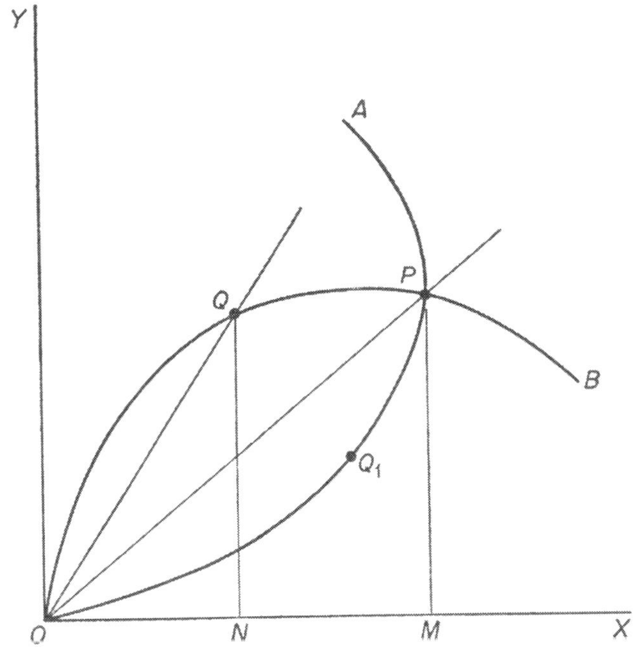


DIAGRAM II

parties will be able to move without bringing the other down to a less preferred position.

(b) If the bargain is made as a whole—if, that is to say, the exchange takes place as a single transaction from the position $O$, then the range of contract will lie on the double curve $QPQ_1$, which is called the *bargaining locus*, $Q$ and $Q_1$ being points which represent the extreme most favourable bargains for $A$ and $B$ respectively. If $A$ is the stronger bargainer, he will be able to bring $B$ over to a point near to $Q$. On the other hand, if $B$ is the stronger bargainer, exchange will take place at a point nearer to $Q_1$.

In either of the circumstances considered above, equilibrium is indeterminate. In either case, all we know is the range over which the equilibrium will lie; we cannot know its precise position. However, in case (b), if at all the rate of interchange given by the relative bargaining strength of the two parties were known, the amounts of $X$ and $Y$ exchanged could be read off from the relevant offer curve. In so far as the whole transaction is completed in a single bargain, a definite volume of trade will be associated with a given rate of interchange. For example, taking the extreme most favourable rate for $A$ to prevail, namely tan $\angle QOX$, it can be seen from Diagram II that the amount of $X$ exchanged will be $ON$ and the amount of $Y$ exchanged will be $QN$. In case (a), on the other hand, even if the final rate of interchange were known, the other variables would still be unknown. Here the equilibrium process leads up through a series of exchanges to a final position. But the final rate does not provide a clue to the earlier rates, nor for the matter of that to amounts of $X$ and $Y$ exchanged. However—and this is the crucial point—if somehow the parties hit upon the rate represented by the co-ordinates of the point $P$ where the two offer curves intersect, and if this rate were adhered to throughout the course of exchange, then the market would close at $P$ and the volume of trade could be derived from the rate of interchange. The same result would follow if the parties had equal bargaining strength and their pressure were such as to bring the equilibrium position over to $P$, In such circumstances tan $\angle POX$ would be the rate of interchange and $OM$ and $PM$ would be the amount of $X$ and $Y$ exchanged respectively.

Edgeworth invokes the hypothesis of what he calls 'recontract' to explain determinateness of equilibrium. In so far as earlier contracts can be revised as equilibrium price is approached, no transaction need actually take place at prices other than the equilibrium price. And if the scope of recontract is so wide that the ultimate equilibrium takes place at $P$, then we have a situation which has just been contemplated, namely one in which the amount of $X$ exchanged, the amount of $Y$ exchanged and the price ratio between the two are all derived from the point of intersection of the offer curves. This condition, according to Edgeworth, is fulfilled under perfect competition. When there are a large number of buyers and sellers (holders of $X$ and $Y$ in our example), a large scope is opened up for recontract and the range of final contract is narrowed down, until in the limit it gets down to the point at which the offer curves interest.

So far so good. But is this a realistic hypothesis? Does it typify the operation of the market as we know it? Marshall does not believe it does, and would not dismiss the possibility of transactions at prices other than the equilibrium price. The device that Marshall employs in this connexion is well-known. He concentrates on each single money-commodity transaction and assumes that the marginal utility of money is constant. This means, when money is measured along the *Y*-axis and the commodity along the *X*-axis, that the contract curve is a vertical line passing through the point of intersection of the offer curves. On this assumption the final price of the commodity turns out to be determinate whatever the initial price and the intermediate prices at which transactions are held. Yet even here the equilibrium point gives us only the amount of the *commodity* bought and sold; it does not give us the amount of *money* that is transferred from the buyers to the sellers in the course of transactions. The situation still eludes the apparatus of our offer curves; we know the measure of *X*, but we do not know the measure of *Y*.

Let us examine this with reference to the famous corn-market example of Marshall.[1] The demand and supply of corn in terms of money are set forth in the following table.

| *At the price* | *Sellers are willing to sell* | *Buyers are willing to buy* |
|---|---|---|
| 37s per quarter | 1000 quarters | 600 quarters |
| 36s per quarter | 700 quarters | 700 quarters |
| 35s per quarter | 600 quarters | 900 quarters |

The table shows that for 700 quarters of corn the marginal rate of preference for corn in terms of money is the same for both the parties; and since the marginal utility of money is constant, this rate (1:36) is independent of the amount of money that the buyers part with and the sellers receive in the course of trade. Thus whatever route the market may take—whether it starts with 35s per quarter or with 37s per quarter—trading will stop at the 700th quarter and at that point the price will be 36s per quarter, any other price being unacceptable either to the buyers or to the sellers. We have the equilibrium price at 36s per quarter and the amount of corn bought and sold at 700 quarters. But our apparatus breaks down when we come to considering the other variable—the amount of money that is transferred from the buyers to the sellers in the process of exchange; for that is something which in the circumstances cannot be read off from the demand and supply schedules. Obviously more money will pass from the buyers to the sellers if the sellers are the shrewder bargainers and the market starts with a price nearer to 37s per quarter than if it were the other way about and the market started with a price nearer to 35s per quarter. What difference this makes depends upon how far away these 'false' prices (as Hicks would call them) are from the equilibrium price and how much trade takes place at these prices.

[1] *Principles of Economics* (London, 7th edition, 1916), Book V, Chapter II.

## III

Once, however, we leave off the narrow region of the daily market and go over to what Marshall calls the normal problem, the situation becomes different. Abstracting for the moment from the problem of 'production', we may assume, for example, that stocks are cleared each day in our corn market and the dealers resume operation the next day with the same conditions of demand and supply confronting them. It is then reasonable to expect that with past experience at their back they will start straight with equilibrium price and adhere to it throughout. Yesterday's closing price will be the basis of today's bargain, and the market will settle down to the equilibrium level where, if we still pursue our corn-market example, 700 quarters of corn will be bought and sold each day at 36s per quarter. But what does this come to? Is it not just the problem of normal 'flow' that Marshall speaks of? The unit of time is a day; and we have the equilibrium flow of corn cleared through the market per unit of time, the price per quarter at which it is bought and sold *and* the flow of money going over to the sellers—all derived from the demand and supply curves. Now of course, given time, there arises the problem of production and its repercussion upon supply. The normal problem includes production, and normal supply curve is a function of the reservation demand of producers for resources just as the market supply curve is a function of the reservation demand of sellers for the community. But this complication, despite its importance from the point of view of the analysis of the supply curve itself, does not affect our immediate problem of the determinateness of equilibrium.

We now know why Marshall had less compunction in using demand and supply curves in the context of the *normal* problem. The normal problem relates to a 'flow' over time. And in so far as, given time, the buyers and sellers can acquire knowledge of the conditions of the market the price that *tends to persist* is determinate and so is the rate of consumption and production *that tends to be maintained* per unit of time provided that—and this is the implication of what Marshall calls the 'statical method'—*other things remain the same.*

Can this interpretation be generalized so as to cover the barter case which, in its normal aspect, typifies Marshall's analysis of International Values? There seems to be no reason why it could not be. If Edgeworth's 'recontract' implies, as it does in essence, a process of acquisition of knowledge of the conditions of the market, there is no reason why just this principle could not be extended to explain determinateness of *normal* equilibrium in the barter case. Indeed there seems to be little doubt that this is what Marshall does in his study of International Values. He considers the case of International Trade as if it is a case of barter where goods are exchanged for goods. This rules out the constant marginal utility assumption that he employs in his analysis of Domestic Values. And yet, relying simply on the assumption of 'free competition', he proceeds with the hypothesis that equilibrium is in all respects determinate. In his example of trade between England and Germany,[1] the intersection of the respective offer curves of the two countries *OE* and *OG* (similar to *OA* and *OB* in our diagrams) is shown to indicate not only the rate of interchange between *E*-goods and *G*-goods but also the equilibrium exports (or imports) of *E*-goods *as well* as *G*-goods. A little 'trial and error' is allowed if the trade is new. But such trading at 'false' prices is left out in the context of the normal flow of the goods interchanged.[2] And it is in this context that Marshall considers the use of demand and supply curves to be appropriate and meaningful.

[1] See *Money, Credit and Commerce* (London, 1923), Appendix J; also *Pure Theory of Foreign Trade* (London School of Economics Reprint).

[2] 'A little "trial and error" may be necessary if the trade is new: But when matters have settled down and experience have been gained, the amount of *E*'s goods sent to *G* will be such that the terms on which *G* will accept them, will cause just that amount of *G*'s goods to be returned to *E* which *E* is willing to accept on those terms.' *Money, Credit and Commerce*, p. 164. Contrast this with the analysis of the apple-nut case where care is taken to show that equilibrium is indeterminate. *Principles* (7th edition), Appendix F on Barter, particularly the last paragraph on p. 792, where the analysis is apparently extended to conditions of free competition.

# 12

# THE THEORY OF BLACK MARKET PRICES*

## I

The essential function of the price mechanism is the smooth clearance of the available supply of an economic good in a market. An economic good is a good whose supply is scarce in relation to demand—'scarcity' implying simply that the entire want of the society is not satisfied by the available supply. In view of the scarcity of supply, buyers press against one another, and those who fail to offer the ruling price in the market go unsatisfied. Price thus measures the strength of excluded demand—being determined by the degree of scarcity of supply relatively to the market demand. In a free price system, excess demand or excess supply tends automatically to be corrected. Excess demand is a signal for a price rise, and excess supply is a signal for a price fall. Competition among buyers and sellers brings it about that a price is settled in the market at which demand is equated to the supply. The available supply is taken off the market by those buyers who are relatively stronger and are prepared to offer the ruling price; those who cannot afford to pay the ruling price go unsatisfied.

The price at which demand is equated to the supply is called by economists the normal price. In a free market, demand and supply forces can be relied on to secure the establishment of a normal price and to ensure the smooth disposal of a commodity. Each has the right to bid his own price for the commodity that he wants, and if the price offered satisfies the seller, the deal is finished without more ado. On the other hand, however intense the need that he may feel for a commodity, it remains unsatisfied unless it is backed by the power to pay a price which will satisfy the seller. The free price system is thus a delicate mechanism through which are avoided all kinds of manoeuvrings that would otherwise appear in the society as a result of the pressure of demand upon scarce supply.

Yet there is one limitation of the free price system, however satisfactory it might be in respect of the smooth delivery of goods. The system caters to the wants of stronger members of the society at the expense of its weaker members. And, since this strength is permitted to express itself in terms of the capacity to pay, the

* Originally published in *The Economic Weekly*, Annual Number, January, 1950.

distribution of a good, as it takes place through the market mechanism, turns out to be in accordance with the relative income of buyers rather than with their relative needs. And in a society which is characterized by large inequalities of income, this certainly proves to be a serious limitation.

This is the sanction for price control. If the normal price is found too high for the poorer section of the community and if it is felt that they should also be allowed to have a share of the available supply of a commodity, the State comes forward and fixes a legal maximum for the market price. A price below 'normal' is fixed and sellers are coerced into accepting what is deemed to be the maximum allowable, consistently with the demand coming from the relatively poor.[1] A price fixed below normal does bring the controlled good within the reach of the hitherto unsatisfied buyers, although in doing so it deprives the stronger buyers of a share that would, in the absence of control, belong to them. If the control is judiciously and effectively administered, it may lead to a more desirable distribution of the available supply.

There is, however, one aspect of the matter which must not be lost sight of. The limitation of the free price system that we have mentioned arises out of large inequalities of income. It is because of this inequality that the normal price fails to satisfy the general need of the society to the extent deemed desirable. Now if this problem of inequality can be tackled directly, through taxes and subsidies, or through other measures of general income control, the case for price control surely disappears. If the income ratio between different groups in the society is brought down to the level that is considered desirable, the free price system surely comes into its own. In principle, indeed, this is a surer way of achieving the objective that we have in view. Whereas an overall income control relieves the State of the necessity of looking into individual markets, the principle of price control, since it relates to individual markets, requires a wider and a more extended supervision, its nature depending upon the character of the market and the number of commodities to be controlled.

What happens if the price of a commodity is fixed by the State at a level below what it would be under the free play of the forces of demand and supply? A state of 'excess demand' is created; sellers offer to sell a quantity which falls short of that which the buyers are willing to buy at the given price. The market thus experiences 'shortage'—a phenomenon, which is to be distinguished from 'scarcity' proper. For, whereas 'scarcity' denotes merely that some demand is excluded because the buyers cannot afford to pay the

[1] The opposite case—that of fixing a minimum price—is not relevant to our present problem and is therefore ruled out.

ruling price, 'shortage' indicates that even those buyers who are willing to pay a price acceptable to the sellers may have to go unsatisfied. Scarcity is ubiquitous in the exchange economy; the fact that a price is to be paid at all is an indication that scarcity exists. Shortage, on the other hand, is the outcome of an artificial control which puts a brake on supply but at the same time releases a demand which otherwise would remain subdued.

How is this short supply distributed among the intending buyers? Does it go to those who come first, or to those who are physically stronger and can push others out of the market? Obviously any such process would frustrate the object of price control. The technique of rationing is thus the essential corollary of a system of price control. The controlling authority undertakes to arrange a distribution of whatever supply is available at the legal price among the intending buyers according to their relative needs. This obviously means that, although people 'at the bottom of the scale' get a part of their demand satisfied, those at the upper end of the scale are asked to accept a ration smaller than what, with their stronger purchasing power, they could secure in a free market by bidding up prices. Here, therefore, are buyers eager to pay higher prices for an extra supply and sellers equally eager to switch on to the stronger market if only such a market can be created. Thus the emergence of the so-called 'black market' is the inevitable consequence of price control and rationing. Because there are buyers prepared to buy at higher prices more than their ration coupons allow, and because there are sellers to whom the commercial code rather than the law of the land is supreme, and who are, therefore, anxious to sell their good to the highest bidder, an area tends inevitably to develop over which transactions take place at prices higher than the legal maximum—its extent depending upon the degree of supervision exercised by the state towards the enforcement of law.

## II

How are black market prices determined? Do they tend to be lower than the normal price as it would be in a free market? What tends to be the output of a commodity that finds its way into black markets? Does it exceed or fall short of the normal output? This is a new field of enquiry which has opened up in the wake of war and post-war price controls and rationing. For, since these controls have been introduced, black markets have been a common phenomenon almost everywhere.

Not enough has yet been done, it appears, by our economists to analyse the affairs of the black markets. We have had a lot of discussion concerning the difficulties arising from the heterogeneity of products within the same industry, differences in the costs of different firms, vagueness of the needs of consumers, etc. We have also been told about the possible failure of price control measures in view of the illegal transactions that 'shortages' would inevitably call forth. But the actual operations of the black markets, in spite of their wide prevalence, have been left practically alone.

But not entirely. Kenneth E. Boulding's *Economic Analysis* contains an ingenious theory of black market prices, although even here, as the present paper purports to show, the matter has been presented in too *simpliste* a fashion and the essential character of the phenomenon has been lost sight of. The following diagram is the basis of Boulding's analysis.[1]

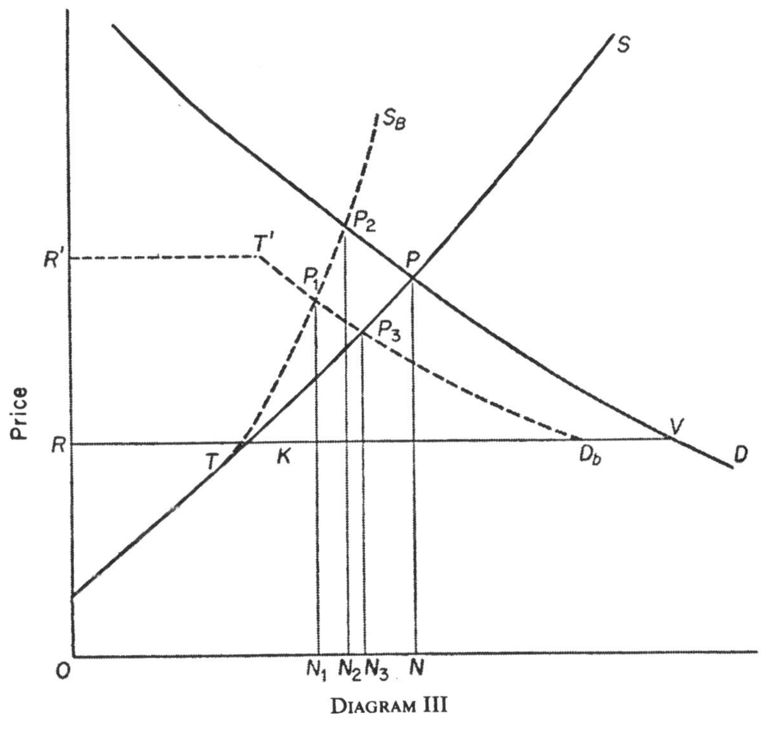


DIAGRAM III

*D* and *S* represent the normal demand and supply curves as they would be in the absence of control. *PN* would then be the normal price, and *ON* the amount bought and sold. If, now, *OR* is fixed by the State to be the maximum price at which buying and selling are legally allowed, the quantity supplied comes down to *RT* and the

[1] Cf. Boulding, *Economic Analysis* (Revised edition, London, 1948), pp. 153–5.

quantity demanded goes up to *RV*. To relieve the congestion of demand the commodity is rationed. But since the available supply in the legal market is only *RT*, many willing buyers go unsatisfied, and an illegal market develops.

What are the demand and supply conditions in this illegal market? Here is Boulding's own story: 'We can postulate a "black market supply curve", $TS_B$ lying to the left of the normal supply curve *TS*. As operations in the black market involve a certain cost and risk above what would be necessary in a free market, suppliers are not to be found willing to supply as much at each price in the black market as would be done in the free market; in other words, because of the higher costs it now takes a higher price to call forth any given quantity than it did before. The higher the costs of black market operation, the steeper will $TS_B$ rise. We can similarly postulate a black market demand curve, $T'D_b$. Even at the legal maximum price (*OR*) we may suppose that not all potential buyers are willing to buy in the black market so that the quantity demanded in the black market at the price *OR* is not the total unsatisfied demand quantity, *TV*, but a smaller quantity $TD_b$ . . . Then the black market price is $P_1 N_1$, and the quantity bought and sold in the black market is *TK*, *RK* being the total quantity in the legal and the black market combined, and *RT* the quantity in the legal market.' It is further argued that in case there are no penalties of any kind, legal or moral, attached to purchases in the black market, the black market demand curve will be the same as the normal demand curve, $DP_2$, so that, with *TSB* as the black market supply curve, the black market price will be as high as $P_2 N_2$. On the other hand, if suppliers are unmolested and penalties are placed only on black market buyers, the black market price will be as low as $P_3 N_3$.

Boulding derives the following conclusions from his analysis of the black market:

First, the black market price may be less than the normal price as it would be in a free market; $P_1N_1$, as the diagram shows, is less than *PN*. Secondly, the average price in the legal and the black market together is likely to be less than the normal price, so that 'even if a black market develops as a result of price control the resulting average price is less than that which would have obtained in a perfectly free market.' And, thirdly, the more rigorous are the measures taken against the black market buyers the lower is the black market price, and the larger the penalties placed on sellers, the higher is the black market price—the inference from this being that 'other things being equal, it would be better to penalize the buyers rather than the sellers in the black market, the housewife rather than the grocer.'

## III

While the above analysis raises certain interesting issues, the manner in which the problem is handled leaves room for further reflection. In general, the extension of demand and supply curves, such as is done, to cover the black market area is not only logically untenable, it is also misleading in its implications. To an examination of this we shall now turn.

In the first place, it is wrong to take the unobstructed black market demand curve to be just an extension of the original *D*-curve. It must be remembered that, according to hypothesis, the legal supply *RT*, is sold at the controlled price, *OR*, and is thus open to buyers within the range *PV* equally with the buyers belonging to the upper range. If, then, a part of the amount sold in the legal market is taken away by buyers lying in the range *TV*, the demand curve in the black market, in the absence of penalties, gets shifted above $DP_2$. The stronger buyers within the range *RT*, with part of their demand unsatisfied, assert themselves in the black market and offer a price which is higher than is shown in the original demand curve. Neglecting obstacles to demand, therefore, the point $T^1$ invariably lies vertically above the *D*-curve.

As regards the black market supply curve, if risks attend black market selling, this curve should lie above the *S*-curve over its whole length, the distance between the two curves depending upon the marginal risk-cost associated with increasing sales in the black market. If the marginal risk-cost remains constant, the two curves will be parallel. If, on the other hand, as is more likely, the sellers are afraid that extension of sales in the black market will involve wider publicity and increasing risk of detection, the distance between the two curves will grow wider as they move to the right. In any case, the initial point on the black market supply curve will be vertically above *T*. Further, the amount sold in the legal market will depend not only upon average cost, as is assumed in the diagram, but also upon the degree of restriction that is placed upon black market selling. *RT* is certainly the maximum amount that can be sold at the controlled price, *OR*. Yet it may not be the actual amount released in the open market at that price, since the black markets would promise a higher return. To what extent output which could profitably be sold in the legal market would nevertheless disappear into the dark area will depend upon the rigour with which black market dealings are treated.

Thirdly—and this is by far the most important point about the whole matter—the so-called black market is a bundle of isolated transactions which, strictly speaking, do not form a market at all.

The illegal character of the transactions naturally precludes the possibility of that degree of intercommunication between buyers and sellers which makes for a perfect market with a uniform price. By its very nature, the black market, such as it is, is at best an imperfect institution in which individual buyers and sellers are, so to say, paired, and separate prices tend to evolve in respect of the same commodity—the level in each case depending upon the relative strength of the parties. To talk of *the* black market price, determined at the point of intersection between the black market demand and supply curves, is thus illegitimate. Indeed the theory that is relevant here is rather that of imperfect market and discrimination, and the technique that is appropriate is that of marginal revenue and marginal cost. The intersection between the black market demand and supply curves may point to a minimum price at which a parcel of product *might* be sold profitably, due account being taken of the risks of such sales; it does not indicate the average price at which the black market output is *actually* sold. Thus even if the black market supply curve cuts the black market demand curve at $P_1$ (as shown in the diagram), the amount bought and sold in the area will not be necessarily $ON_1$, nor will the average price be necessarily $P_1N_1$. Since some degree of discrimination will be possible, the average revenue curve will surely lie above $T'D_b$.

## IV

What does all this lead to? How are our generalizations concerning black markets affected by these considerations?

In the first place, since the black market area is dominated by stronger buyers and since, in the absence of intercommunication, sellers, strengthened by the fact of shortage, are in a position to apply discrimination to their advantage, the average of prices within the black market area (which, according to our hypothesis, exceeds the marginal demand price) tends to be higher than the normal price as it would be in a free market. The reverse may happen only if very high penalties are placed upon black market buyers.

Secondly, the average price in the legal and the black markets taken together, depending, as it does, upon the level of controlled price, the level of black market prices and the area covered by illegal transactions relatively to the open market, may easily exceed the normal free market price. This tendency becomes all the more likely if control over black market dealings is slackened; for, in that case, a larger proportion of the aggregate output goes into the black market area. Thus an act of concession to black market sellers, while it may bring down black market prices as such, is altogether not certain in its effect on average price in the combined area, when account is taken of its repercussion on the volume of output available for the 'open' area.

Thirdly, since, if the law is to be taken at all seriously, the objective of policy must be to stop black market dealings, or, at any rate, to reduce their area to the minimum, it is a matter of indifference whether buyers or sellers or both are chosen for punishment in respect of these dealings. For it is just a question of keeping the demand curve below the supply curve in the black market region. And this of course can be done either by pushing down the demand curve through penalties on buyers or by pushing up the supply curve through penalties on sellers. Either of these operations, if carried on successfully, would serve the purpose equally well. It is for the State to decide which would be more convenient and more effective from the administrative point of view.

Lastly—given the black market supply curve, the higher the penalties placed on illegal buying the lower surely is the average of prices, but the smaller also is the output sold in the black market. If, then, consumers' surplus is taken to be the criterion of gain to buyers—to estimate which penalties, both actual and potential, as also the loss of output available, are to be taken into account—it is misleading, under the pretext of price reduction, to make a scapegoat of the buyer.

These considerations suggest the sort of dilemma to which a policy of price control and rationing gives rise. If control over the black market is slackened, aggregate output expands, but the legal market is left high and dry, and the scheme of rationing is endangered. On the other hand, if control over the black market is tightened, the supply in the legal market expands, but the aggregate output shrinks, and there is damage to consumer's surplus.

*Note.*—This is with reference to para. 2, section III, above. On re-reading the passage I notice a certain obscurity in my formulation which needs removal.

The point made out there is that when a part of the legal market output is shared by buyers who, if it were a free market, would not have access to it, the black market demand curve takes a position above the normal demand curve. To see why it does, take a point $Q$ on the $D$-curve, vertically above $T'$ (Diagram III). Draw $QM$ perpendicular to the horizontal axis (not shown in the diagram). Now $QM$ is the price offered by stronger buyers in a free market for output $OM$ (or $RT$). If, however, in view of price control, they are deprived of a part of $OM$, then at $M$ where the actual amount that they buy is less than $OM$, their demand price is greater than $QM$. If $Q'M$ ($Q'M > QM$) is the demand price that corresponds to this amount, then $Q'$ is on the black market demand curve, as it would be without risks of punishment.

# 13

# PLANNED ECONOMIC DEVELOPMENT AND RELATIVE PRICES*

## I

Let me state a theory of price variations in the context of an economy having a process of planned economic development. Assume, first, that the additional investment, both in the public sector and in the private sector, is matched entirely by taxation and voluntary savings. Assume, too, that the period under consideration is too short for the output of consumption goods to increase with the increase in the outlay on investment. On these assumptions the aggregate expenditure on consumption remains the same and, since the output also remains the same, there is a sense in which it can be said that the general price level remains constant. Employment in the investment goods sector no doubt increases; so does the total wage bill in this sector. But the additional expenditure on consumption on this account is just neutralized by the curtailment of consumption done by the rest of the community.

The general price level may even fall under the condition postulated if the period chosen is long enough for some of the investment projects to be completed and to start yielding consumption goods. For, the output of consumption goods increases during the period, while the aggregate expenditure remains the same. This, incidentally, is a situation in which, if money wage rate is held constant, as indeed is our assumption, labour gets the full benefit of its increased productivity resulting from the additional investment. If in such circumstances, the general price level is to be kept stable, a part of the additional investment has to be financed by deficit, i.e. by pushing the additional wage bill in the investment goods sector beyond what is warranted by the additional savings of the community.

This indeed is the *raison d'être* of deficit financing in the context of planned economic development of an under-developed country. Deficit financing, however, generates a rise in the general price level if pushed further up so as to outrun the increase in the output of consumption goods during any planning period. The deficit may

* Memorandum submitted to the Foodgrains Enquiry Committee, Government of India, 1957. Originally published in *The Economic Weekly*, December 7, 1957.

occur in the private sector as much as it can occur in the public sector. It is customary to relate deficit financing to Budget deficit. But, in fact, from the point of view of 'social accounting', deficit in the private sector is as significant as deficit in the public sector. Whereas the latter manifests itself in an expansion of currency coming via sale of Treasury Bills to the Central Bank, the former manifests itself in an expansion of credit coming via sale of commercial bills and mortgage of other assets to the commercial banks. The two have the same kind of impact upon the economy, and they can, and often do, operate at the same time.

All this when the matter is looked at in the aggregate; when, that is to say, reference is made to what is called the 'general price level'. What happens to 'relative prices'? In our anxiety to bring out the broad effect of investment and saving upon the economy as a whole, we often forget the affairs of individual markets and the forces that govern the movement of individual prices. In the short period at any rate—which is the period that is relevant when we talk of Five Year Plans—there is no reason why individual prices should move in the way the general price level moves. This is common knowledge, and yet the matter has become particularly significant from the point of view of planned economic development where the pattern of investment is controlled with a view to certain long term objectives and is not adjusted to short term profits. In fact, it should be possible, in the context of economic planning, to read off from the pattern of investment relatively to the consumption propensities of individual groups in the society how the various markets are to be affected by the Plan during any given period.

Imagine the extreme case where planned investment is fully matched by planned saving, and the flow of output of consumption goods of various kinds remains more or less constant. Employment increases in the investment goods sector. But, since at the initial stage of planning there is unemployment, both open and disguised, this increase is not at the expense of employment in the consumption goods sector. The newly employed labourers in the investment goods sector are paid at the current rate of wages prevailing in the economy. The additional expenditure done by the newly employed labourers is, however, neutralized by the curtailment of expenditure through saving done by the rest of the community. The general price level, of course, remains the same. But, unless the pattern of saving is such that expenditure is curtailed by the rest of the community on just those goods on which the extra expenditure of the newly employed labourers has its impact, individual prices do move in different directions. Some prices rise and some prices fall.

This aspect of the matter is often overlooked when attention is fixed on total investment and total saving. In fact, in practice, savings, including taxes paid to the Government, come from people who could ordinarily afford to buy luxury or near-luxury goods. And when they are asked to save more or to pay more taxes, they tend naturally to curtail the consumption of these goods. On the other hand, the people (mostly labourers) to whom the money thus saved is transferred via the investors, are more prone to spend on necessaries. Thus, though the total expenditure in money terms remains more or less constant, the prices of necessaries—wage goods, that is to say—tend to rise and the prices of non-wage goods tend to fall. Food happens to be the most important item in the labourers' budget. It has also an inelastic demand, so far as the budget of the rest of the community is concerned. Whereas, therefore, increased employment in the investment good sector leads to an increased demand for goods, there is no corresponding curtailment of its consumption on the part of those from whom savings come. It is thus inevitable that food prices should rise in the process of planned economic development unless provision is made in the Plan itself to increase the supply of food (either through internal production or through imports) *pari passu* with increasing investment involving increasing employment of labour.

Imagine, on top of this, a dose of deficit-financing. If this happens, the general price level rises, but the prices of wage goods rise more than in proportion to the rise in the general price level. Further, even if the output of various consumption goods rises during the Plan period, the same tendency operates if the volume of deficit-financing exceeds what is often called the 'safety limit'. Relative prices do get distorted, the reaction in individual markets depending upon the expenditure pattern of the community relatively to the supply of individual goods.

## II

I have stated this theory of price variations rather elaborately because it appears to me that certain features of our present situation fit it very closely and I suspect that not enough attention has been given to this aspect of the matter. In the course of the implementation of the Second Five Year Plan, during the last one year and a half, the general price level has risen substantially, though not beyond anticipation, food prices have risen very much more than in proportion to the rise in the general price level, and the prices of manufactures very much less. To fix our mind on the degree of price variations, it may be noted that during the first year of the Plan (July 1956 to July 1957), the general price level rose by about 8 per cent, while the price of rice rose by a little over 13 per cent and of wheat by a little over 11 per cent. The prices of manufactures, on the other hand, rose by just about 4 per cent.

The rise in the general price level is due to the over-all deficit financing (including investment in the private sector) that has occurred in the economy toward the closing stage of the First Five Year Plan and the first year of the Second Five Year Plan. The deficit in the public sector has no doubt been more or less neutralized by balance of payments deficit; between July 1956 and July 1957 the increase in note circulation has been of the order of Rs 55 crores. Yet, on this is superimposed an enormous volume of private investment as indicated by an increase in bank advances of the order of Rs 142 crores. It is, however, misleading in this context to isolate the Budget deficit from over-investment in the private sector too sharply. For if there had been less investment in the private sector there would correspondingly be less deficit in the balance of payments. Consequently, there would be a larger expansion of currency and the impact of budget deficit would be more conspicuous. From the social accounting point of view—which is the point of view that is relevant here—what is significant is the overall deficit in the economy as a whole.

The distortion of the price structure with a bias towards higher food prices is surely the consequence of the change in the expenditure pattern along the lines indicated in the analysis presented above. The output of rice and wheat increased to some extent (about 5 per cent) during the years 1955–6 and 1956–7. But the increase in output was more than offset by the increase in expenditure resulting, on the one hand, from overall deficit financing and, on the other hand, from a shift of demand which affected food more than anything else.

Ordinarily, the effect of investment and saving is not analysed in terms of 'relative prices' in the way it has been done here because, first, it is thought that although in the short period such distortions may take place, given time they are evened out, and, secondly a temporary short-fall in the supply of food can be covered by imports. The first argument is not relevant in the context of a planned economy where the Plan itself is industry-biased, as it is here so far as our Second Plan is concerned. In fact, in a planned economy, the Plan itself might be framed in a manner such as would look after the possible distortions in the demand structure in the process of growth, so that the so-called long period result might be achieved at each stage of planning. But, this is not the pattern in which the present Plan has been set; deliberately emphasis has been placed on industry. Yet, the second consideration still remains, namely, that of covering shortages by imports. Indeed in the present context food import assumes a priority as high as that of the import of capital goods. Food is as much a capital good as it is a consumption good. Economists would rank it as 'circulating capital' alongside of, and complementary to, 'fixed capital' in the context of economic development.

If the analysis given above is correct, then several conclusions follow:

(i) The situation on the food front is not so alarming, nor is it so unexpected, as it is often made out to be. There may be spatial imbalances of a serious magnitude. But that is a problem of distribution.

(ii) The factors that have led to the rise of food prices are by and large healthy, for they are indicators of economic growth.

(iii) Increased employment which must have accompanied the process of investment, whether in the public sector or in the private sector, has to be set at least as partial compensation against the rise in food prices.

(iv) We should not have much qualm about raising the import bill for food, when necessary. For example, full utilization of P L 480 seems to be warranted in the present circumstances

It will be seen that the present Memorandum has sought just to provide an analytical framework in terms of which the problem of food prices might be judged in the context of economic development. Special problems connected with internal production, release of marketable surplus, the possible need for control and rationing, etc., have been left out of consideration.

I may only add, again if the analysis given here is correct, that we should be prepared for a continuation of the process that we are experiencing at the moment if our Plans move along the present line with its bias towards industry and with the method of financing maintained as it is.

# 14

# THE CHOICE OF TECHNIQUE*

## I

When factor prices are given and constant—as they are supposed to be to a firm under theoretically perfect competition—and factor proportions are variable, you choose that combination of factors in production which equates the relative prices of factors to their relative marginal productivity. The object is to minimize cost of a given output. The combination that you choose gives you the technique of production. The prices of factors depend upon their relative degree of scarcity. If labour is more scarce relatively to capital, you choose a relatively capital-intensive technique. If, on the other hand, capital is more scarce than labour, you choose a relatively labour-intensive technique. The production function, together with factor prices, solves the problem of choice of technique.

Let us be clear about the assumption that we are making here. The output is given, and the same given output can be produced by varying proportions of capital and labour. You may use a little less of labour and a little more of capital, or you may use a little more of labour and a little less of capital, and yet you will get the same output. There is, however, one particular proportion which satisfies the minimum cost condition, and it is this proportion that you choose. The technique thus is independent of the scale of production.

Now vary the hypothesis and assume that the volume of capital—howsoever it might be measured—is given, while labour is variable at constant price. Here the output will vary with every variation in the labour-capital ratio, i.e. with every variation in the technique of production. In what manner? Applying the so-called law of non-proportional returns, one finds that with given capital and varying labour employment, the output goes on increasing up to a point and then declines. Over a range, increasing labour-capital ratio yields increasing returns. But beyond a point, there is too much of labour used with relatively too little of capital and you have the phenomenon of 'diminishing returns'. Where do you fix your technique in this case? Applying the principle of minimum cost, you choose that technique where the wage rate is equal to the marginal product of labour. If you make your technique more labour-intensive, although your total output may increase, the wage rate exceeds the marginal product and, therefore, the average labour-cost of output increases.

* Originally published in *The Economic Weekly*, Special Number, July, 1958.

In both these cases the criterion of choosing the technique is the same—the criterion of minimum cost, which is the only valid economic criterion. However, whereas in the former case, since the output to be derived is given and the problem of technique is a problem of the *substitution* of labour for capital, the pertinent equation is the equation between *relative* factor prices and relative marginal product—in the latter case, since the volume of available capital is given, so that capital figures as Ricardian land, the relevant equation is the equation between the price of the variable factor, labour, and its marginal product.

Now, it is this latter hypothesis which forms the basis of recent discussions on the choice of technique. The discussion arose first in the context of the reconstruction of war-devastated economies and then extended to the problem of planned development of under-developed economies. These economies have two things in common —a plethora of unemployed labour and a limited supply of capital. The aggregate of this capital is composed in varying proportions of foreign aid (Marshall Aid, for example) and internal savings. It is reasonable to assume in the context of these economies that, while the form in which capital is to be used is variable, the volume of capital as such is not. Since, therefore, the form which the given capital is allowed to assume determines the amount of labour that a unit of capital can accommodate at full capacity, the question naturally arises as to how labour-intensive (or capital-intensive) the technique of production should be—what, in other words, should be the amount of labour employed per unit of capital with reference to the varying forms that the available capital might be given. The problem is complicated by the fact that there exists in such economies a plethora of unemployed labour, so that the supply of labour is perfectly elastic as much to the economy as a whole as it is supposed to be to a firm under perfect competition.

## II

The answer given to the question by the post-war economic theorists who have worked in this field has been based on alternative criteria of policy. I shall take two of these criteria which have figured rather more conspicuously—the criteria of maximum surplus and maximum output, and see what they precisely mean. For my purpose, which is just illustrative, it is enough if we take the simple, single-product model. Given the volume of capital, the output is a function of the amount of labour employed, i.e. of the labour-capital ratio. Thus, with each technique of production, there is a corresponding output. The form of this function is, however, such that as we go on increasing the labour-capital ratio, the resulting output increases up to a point and then it declines. There is, therefore, a certain labour-capital ratio which corresponds to maximum output.

There are those who argue that, since the opportunity cost of unemployed labour is zero, employment of labour should be carried up to the point of maximum output and the technique adjusted accordingly. This certainly is a point where we have *currently* the highest standard of living for the population. If we go beyond this, we increase employment, but we reduce output at the same time. On the other hand, there is another point where, at given wage rate, the surplus of output over the total wage cost is maximum. The technique which yields maximum surplus is, given a positive wage rate, necessarily less labour-intensive than the technique which yields maximum output. That we should not choose a technique less labour-intensive than the one that yields maximum surplus or that we should discard any technique more labour-intesive than the one which yields maximum output, is agreed on all hands. But as between maximum surplus and maximum output there is, it is held, a real problem of choice. Assuming that the whole of wages is spent on consumption and the whole or a constant proportion of the surplus is invested, it is argued by some that the technique which yields maximum surplus is the one that should be adopted for it makes for maximum rate of growth.

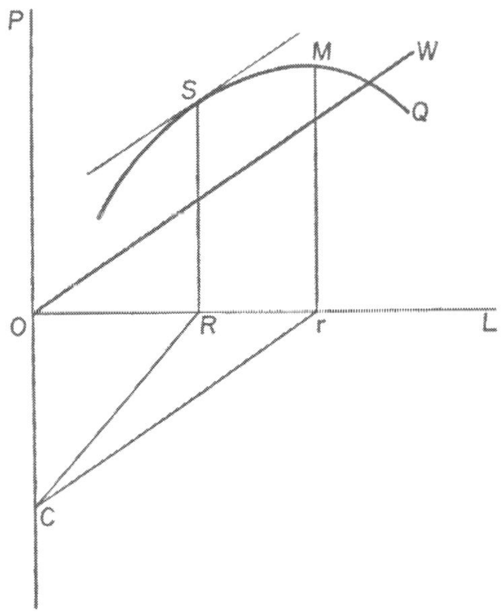


DIAGRAM IV

Let me illustrate the point with reference to a diagram which A. K. Sen employs in this context.[1]

Measure labour along the horizontal axis, *OL*, and product along the vertical axis, *OP*. Suppose the given volume of capital is *OC*, shown below the line, and, with varying degrees of employment of labour, you have the resulting product given by the curve *Q*, which slopes upward up to a point, say, *M*, and then declines. The labour-capital ratio is given by ∠*RCO*, ∠*rCO*, etc., and the corresponding total output is measured by *RS*, *rM*, etc. *OW* is the total wage curve. It is a straight line by hypothesis, for the wage rate (given by ∠*WOL*) is constant. Since the curve *Q* starts sloping downward from *M*, the point, *M*, represents maximum output, while the point, *S*, tangent through which on the *Q*-curve is parallel to *OW*, represents maximum surplus. The corresponding techniques are given by the labour-capital ratios measured by ∠*rCO* and ∠*RCO*. If you are interested in maximizing the current level of income, choose your technique at *M*. If, on the other hand, you want the rate of growth to be maximized and work for a higher income for the future generation, choose your technique at *R*. This is how the problem is usually stated. So sharply are the objectives often contrasted that at least one writer has been led to wonder if the problem posed is a problem of choice of technique at all—if it is not just a choice of objective.[2]

## III

However, the matter may be put somewhat differently so as to conform to our accepted economic criterion. The economist cannot obviously decide on any issue between objectives. But cost-price considerations are surely within his domain. And in this particular context of choosing the technique, we do not need to go beyond these considerations; the enunciation of alternative objectives is beside the point.

The accepted economic criterion for a policy decision is the criterion of minimum cost. Applying this criterion, we might say that, if for producing a commodity, different alternative techniques are available, that technique is to be chosen which conforms to the principle of minimum cost. The condition of minimum cost as regards the kind of hypothesis that we have taken is, as we have seen, an equation between wage rate and the marginal productivity of labour. At what technique would the condition be fulfilled? The real problem lies here, for it depends upon what wage rate we take into account for purposes of our calculation. If we go by the market

[1] A. K. Sen, 'Some Notes on the Choice of Capital-Intensity in Development Planning', *Quarterly Journal of Economics*, November, 1957, p. 575.

[2] D. Ghosh, 'Choice of Technique' in *The Economic Weekly*, Annual Number, January, 1958.

wage rate, which is given by $\angle WOL$, the technique at $R$ is the relevant technique. The marginal product of labour is given by the slope at any point on the $Q$-curve. At $S$ where the tangent is parallel to $OW$, therefore, the marginal product of labour is equal to the price of labour. If, on the other hand, we go by the opportunity cost principle, and equate the price of labour with social cost and further assume, in view of the existence of unemployment, that the social cost of employment is zero, the relevant technique is the technique at $r$, for it is here that the marginal product of labour is also zero.

The point of enquiry, therefore, is not what objective we should choose; the objective is indeed unique, namely to minimize cost. The pertinent enquiry is rather whether we should go by the actual market price of labour or by some 'shadow price' given by the opportunity cost of labour. This problem relates specially to the labour market, for however low the opportunity cost of labour may be, there is a minimum below which the market rate of wages cannot go. Even in a state of acute unemployment, a labourer may not choose to accept a job unless he is paid at the existing wage rate, even though the alternative that he is surrendering is just unwanted leisure and no product.

And yet if we consider the matter from the point of view of society, the market rate of wages ceases to be relevant. What matters from the point of view of social cost is the alternative product displaced in the process of the employment of labour. And if that is *nil*, the point of maximum output coincides with the point of minimum cost.

What happens, however, to 'surplus'—the basis of growth? To answer this question, let us make an extreme assumption. Let us assume that the extra wages of the newly employed labour spent on current consumption are fully compensated by saving done by the rest of the community and that this extra saving, even though a part of it may come via additional taxation, is not accompanied by any loss of product to the society in other directions. On this assumption, since savings result in mere transfer of income, the point of maximum output remains the point of maximum surplus, too. Applying the criterion of minimum cost, we have here at the same time maximum output and maximum surplus. What is more important is that the condition that we are postulating here is fulfilled even if a part of the savings is drawn forcibly through inflation, in so far as the consequent reduction in the real wage rate does not affect efficiency of labour.

This extreme assumption, however, does not apply in practice. Even in a state of unemployment, the employment of labour, if carried far enough, does involve social cost, even if indirectly, through loss of efficiency on the part of the agencies from which savings are drawn. The social cost of employment of labour in an over-populated, under-developed country is surely less than the market rate of wages, but we shall go wrong if we equate it to zero just because there is a plethora of unemployed labour. In choosing our technique of production we must go by a 'shadow price' of labour given by the opportunity cost. But it will be rarely that the criterion of minimum cost will justify the adoption of a technique that would correspond to maximum output.

*Part III*

# FOREIGN BALANCE

# 15

# INTERNATIONAL ECONOMIC IMBALANCE*

## I

Perhaps no matter is more significant today to a student of international economics than the state of imbalance in the level of economic development and the rate of economic growth in the different countries of the world. Particular imbalances in the sphere of trade and payments that have loomed so large in our thinking in the post-War years are no doubt serious, and they have made significant impact upon the structure of international economic relatious. We have witnessed a long period of dollar shortage resulting at one stage in a drastic devaluation of a number of currencies, including our own, and only recently we saw its reversal and a sudden appearance of what may be called a state of dollar abundance. We have experienced inflationary tendencies operating in varying degrees in the different economies of the world, and we have had, associated with all this, large scale discriminatory import restrictions, quota arrangements, exchange controls, etc. These are extraordinary phenomena, and they are threatening to be persistent and obstinate. The International Monetary Fund, which was established in 1946 with the object of creating conditions for a smooth and balanced flow of international trade, has even now to have recourse to a certain waiver clause permitting these restrictions if conditions remained abnormal. And a recent *Currency Yearbook* brought out by the US Currency Expert, Franz Pick, stated that at least sixty out of the ninety-three currencies which his team surveyed are out of gear with the US dollar and require far-reaching adjustments. Normality in international payments is yet very far off.

These particular imbalances are no doubt partly due to the damage to productive capacity and trade channels wrought by the war. But in so far as this were so, they were to pass off with the end of the period of reconstruction and the adjustments of the currencies in conformity with the domestic price levels of the trading countries. There are, in fact, people who think that this is all that there is to the problem of international disequilibrium, who argue that the current imbalances in the sphere of international payments are solely due to dislocations caused by the war and that their persistence is due to

* Inaugural address at the Indian School of International Studies, November 1961. Originally published in *International Studies*, Vol. III, No. 3.

the 'irrational' domestic policies pursued by the various countries of the world. 'Whatever may be the nature of the origin of disequilibrium,' argues Lord Robbins in the context of the post-war problem of dollar shortage, 'there is an important sense in which its *persistence* may be said to be due to monetary or financial causes.' For, as he continues, 'in any position of disequilibrium of this sort [dollar shortage] it is possible to conceive of financial adjustments, either by way of alterations of the volume of expenditure or alterations in the rate of exchange, which would tend to put it right.'[1]

Now this is taking too *simpliste* a view of things. It is true that if, after the period of reconstruction was over and production was restored to the pre-war level, national economic policies throughout the world were permitted to be determined exclusively by considerations of external equilibrium, then the era of discriminatory import restrictions, exchange control and things of that sort would by now be over. But there is no reason why external equilibrium should be the only or even the main concern of an economy and why domestic policies designed to secure fuller employment or more rapid economic development should be considered to be at all 'irrational'. We shall indeed go off on false scent if we do not recognize that the peculiar national economic policies which are so often made the scapegoat in the context of post-war payments disequilibrium are a reflection of a general awareness of a deeper imbalance in international economic relations arising out of varying levels of economic development and varying rates of economic growth in the different countries of the world. It is this deeper imbalance rather than its specific outward manifestations that I propose to discuss in this paper.

## II

Over the last two hundred years or so the world has witnessed tremendous progress in science and technology and a tremendous increase in productive capacity. Man's inventive genius has shown remarkable resilience in meeting the challenge thrown up by an ever-growing population upon limited natural resources. Vast potentialities have opened up for the improvement of man's material conditions. And yet these opportunities have been confined to a small part of the earth's surface; the majority of the inhabitants of the world are still poor by any standard.

Inequalities of wealth and opportunity are ubiquitous in our society. Within national boundaries too, there are large inequalities between regions, between sectors and between classes. Conflicts between labour and capital, between rural and urban sectors and

[1] Lionel Robbins, *Economist in the Twentieth Century* (London, 1954) 50.

between progressive and depressed areas have been almost invariable concomitants of the economic growth of a nation. Nevertheless there has been a certain built-in institutional protection against any excess in these inequalities. Trade unions and similar political and social organizations operating within any democratic State have always resisted cumulative tendencies to inequality by their insistence on wage adjustments, parity prices, grants and subsidies, etc. The result is that the process of what Myrdal calls 'national economic integration'[1] has been in operation in more or less degree wherever economic development of any substantial measure has taken place. 'National economic integration has increasingly been a process of social organization, in the course of which social and economic barriers were abolished and greater equality of opportunity realized. In this process a complex system of interference with the functioning of the price mechanism has played an important role.'[2] It would perhaps be wrong to say of even the more advanced countries that they have altogether succeeded in solving their internal contradictions; if they had done so, the tension in international relations would be very much less than it is today. Yet who will deny that these countries have made enormous progress during the last fifty years or so towards a reduction of regional and group disparities in wealth and power? If the less developed countries are still under the pressure of traditional institutions and cultures and if the movement towards national integration is yet slow in these countries, the awareness is there, thanks at least to imported ideologies, if not to an inner urge.

While, however, the internal conflicts are capable of being resolved —and they *are* being resolved—under the aegis of the State which has a controlling authority over contending parties, international economic integration is yet a far cry. If economic inequalities between regions or groups are tending to be reduced, those between nations are in the process of being accentuated over the years. As Professor Rosenstein-Rodan observes, 'there is no doubt that after a hundred, even a hundred and fifty years of industrial revolutions and great technical progress, the degree of inequality of distribution of income as between different nations is considerably greater today than it was a hundred years or even hundred and fifty years ago.'[3]

In a study of the relative economic position of as many as sixty-four countries, whose national income figures are available, Paul Studenski brings out the enormity of the income inequality that

[1] Gunnar Myrdal, *An International Economy—Problems and Prospects* (New York, 1956), Chapter II, pp. 11–14; also Chapter III, *passim*.

[2] Ibid., p. 4.

[3] P. N. Rosenstein-Rodan, 'International Development of Economically Backward Areas', *International Affairs* (April, 1944), p. 158, as quoted in ibid., f.n., p. 341.

prevails among the nations of the world.[1] The *per capita* income of the United States of America is forty times as high as that of Burma and about thirty times as high as that of India. The average *per capita* income of the nine countries ranking highest in the list is $983 per year and that of the lowest nineteen is $94. Only eleven countries have a *per capita* income above $500 per year; the rest are below that level. Three countries have *per capita* income above $1000 per year, while there are as many as twenty-nine countries having less than $200. Putting the matter in another way, two-thirds of the world's population share only about 15 per cent of the world's wealth, whereas just about 18 per cent of the world's population enjoy about two-thirds of the world's wealth.

## III

These are disturbing revelations. And yet there is nothing in it that is surprising. Division of the world into 'nations' has been the result of a series of historical accidents rather than of set design. And in so far as there is at all any design, it is based on linguistic, racial or similar emotional affiliations rather than on economic viability; the political boundaries of the world are independent of the geographical distribution of material resources. The inhabitants of these separate territories have also different social habits and attitudes. Some are thrifty and enterprising, some are not. Some have the 'will to economize', and some do not have it.[2] These habits and attitudes may be partly natural; but partly also—and perhaps very largely—they are conditioned by material environment itself. It is indeed difficult to understand why the people of the East should have in general an 'other-worldly' attitude in contrast with those of the West. It is more reasonable to believe that all of us have split personalities—one inward-looking and the other more earthy. One has only to travel about a little to know how essentially similar we all are in respect of our conception of values and habits of thought and desire. Acquisition of wealth is a general desire, although it may be tempered in more or less degree by considerations of the non-material values of life—the scale leaning more towards the latter not when you have an overdose of wealth but paradoxically when you have too little of it. 'From him who hath not is taken away even that which he hath.' And when on top of all this, account is taken of the fact that the relatively more resourceful part of the world, after having had an early start at industrialization and economic development, extended its acquisitive sway by manipulation or by conquest

[1] Paul Studenski, *Income of Nations* (New York, 1958).
[2] Arthur Lewis, *Theory of Economic Growth* (London, 1955), Chapter II, *passim*.

over the less developed areas of the world, the economic stagnation of the latter is easily explained.

But could not the widening gulf between the rich and poor countries be stemmed by international trade? If the distribution of resources between nations is uneven and these resources are not mobile, could not this unevenness be rectified by movement of products? It has been the contention of liberal economists since the days of the Industrial Revolution in England that the comparative disadvantage of countries less endowed with capital and enterprise tends to be corrected by trade. The idea is implicit in the classical theory of gains from international trade, and the later reformulation of the theory gives it a more explicit sanction. It is true, these economists admit, that resources are not internationally mobile. 'Home,' says Adam Smith, 'is the centre round which the capital of the inhabitants of every country are continually circulating, and towards which they are always tending.'[1] Yet, in so far as commodities are free to move, poorer countries get relief, through trade, from an undue pressure on scarce resources. The benefit comes in two ways: First, it comes through increasing demand from relatively prosperous countries which raises the price of products and hence the wages of labour in the poorer countries. And secondly, it offers opportunity to the poorer countries to secure cheaper goods produced by superior, capital-intensive techniques in the relatively more prosperous countries. International trade in commodities is supposed to be a substitute for international mobility of factors of production.

Now this is a delusion. On a static view it does appear no doubt that trade reduces international differences in wages, for it permits the poorer countries with relatively abundant labour supply to specialize more and more in labour-intensive industries and to secure in return goods which require a relatively larger use of capital. If India has an abundant supply of labour, and England has a scarce supply of it, trade does make it possible for the former to develop labour-intensive industries beyond the level which its own internal demand would warrant, and to meet the demand for more capital-intensive goods by imports from the latter. India can then specialize in more labour-intensive industries and England in more capital-intensive industries, the process bringing the level of wages in India nearer to the level in England. Indeed, arguing on these lines, it can be shown that, subject to reservations following from transport costs and international differences in the quality of labour, wages should tend to equality in different countries if there be free trade in commodities.

The analysis, however, overlooks certain vital elements in the

[1] Adam Smith, *Wealth of Nations* (2 vols., Everyman's Edition), I, p. 399.

chain of causation, in particular the relative bargaining strength of the poorer countries and the relation of terms of trade to the supply of resources and to economies of production. On a dynamic view, when account is taken of these elements, one can visualize the possibility of a cumulative deterioration in the economic position of under-developed countries once they start with inferior terms of trade, and of a reverse process operating in countries which have been ahead in the race.

There is a passage in Marshall's *Principles of Economics* which brings out the nature of this cumulative process with reference to labour-capital relations:

'It is certain that manual labourers as a class are at a disadvantage in bargaining; and that the disadvantage wherever it exists is likely to be cumulative in its effects. For anything that lowers wages tends to lower the efficiency of the labourer's work, and, therefore, to lower the price which the employer would rather pay than go without that work. The effects of the labourer's disadvantage in bargaining are therefore cumulative in two ways. It lowers his wages; and this lowers his efficiency as a worker, and thereby lowers the normal value of his labour. And in addition it diminishes his efficiency as a bargainer, and thus increases the chance that he will sell his labour for less than its normal value.'[1]

The implication of this analysis is perfectly general; it applies to all exchange relations involving parties with unequal bargaining strength. Substitute 'labour' by 'weaker nations', and 'efficiency' by 'economies of production', and you have the spectacle of a cumulative process operating in the international economic field. Poorer countries, because they are poor, have low bargaining strength. They have, therefore, to accept less favourable terms of trade in their dealings with richer countries. Their investible surplus turns out to be less, and they have to turn more to labour-intensive lines of production which offer less scope for economies of production. The opposite happens in the case of richer countries; and the economic gulf between the two widens.[2] Witness, as a practical example, the case of India *vis-à-vis* England under a régime of free

[1] Alfred Marshall, *Principles of Economics* (London, 7th edition, 1916), p. 569. The sentences are put non-consecutively with a view to bringing out the gist.

[2] See J. R. Hicks, *Essays in World Economics* (Oxford, 1959), Supplementary Note C. Commenting on Samuelson's Factor Price Equalization Theories, Hicks observes: 'There is no tendency to equalization, either between the industrial and non-industrialised, or (what is also very significant) among the non-industrialised themselves.They may be rich or poor, according to their endowment of natural resources. Those which are rich in natural resources can industrialise themselves, if they choose; it is easy for them to accumulate necessary capital. But those who are poor in natural resources have no hope save in industrialisation—and here is their dilemma. A small industrial sector does not develop sufficient economies to make it competitive; a large industrial sector requires so much capital as to be out of reach.' Ibid., p. 269.

trade, as it did exist over not an inconsiderable period of time. Can there be any doubt but that the benefit of trade went more to England than to India?

## IV

International economic inequality is not merely a moral problem; it is also a political problem. Considering how the spirit of nationalism has crippled our vision, it is not surprising that the problem did not so long come out very much in the open. And yet as one thinks of it, one does feel a sense of awkwardness at the scant recognition that social thinkers have given to it. Thinking has concentrated more on group (or class?) inequalities as a national problem. And here, on the broad assumption that the marginal utility of income is greater to the poor than to the rich, economists have often gone to the length of advocating forced transfer of wealth from the rich to the poor. Anyway, as a result of pressures over the years, prevention of concentration of power and reduction of regional or group inequalities of income have been recognized by all civilized States to be a major aspect of national economic policy.

Does not the same principle apply to the international economy? Just because the different nations of the world are independent political units and there is no world government to entertain pressures arising from inequalities, the problem as such is not surely eliminated. Gross inequalities are as bad in the international sphere as they are in the domestic sphere. Pressures to reduce them are called for, too, as much when they relate to the international economy as when they relate to domestic economies.

Politically, the existence of a large under-developed area is a threat to international stability. Poverty brings discontent within these areas and may be itself a source of trouble. This, however, is not so important. For it is unlikely that the weaker nations should be able to carry their discontent far enough. Much more serious is the rivalry among stronger nations as regards the sharing of control over these under-developed markets from which they expect to derive gains through trade and sometimes also through investment. One may not choose to accept a purely economic interpretation of history. Yet it is difficult not to believe that the most important single cause of international conflict is rivalry over the so-called 'sphere of influence'. It is no accident that modern wars—hot or cold—have been the result of conflict, not between weaker nations, nor, strictly, between the weaker nations and stronger nations, but between stronger nations themselves.

We are just becoming dimly aware of this international anomaly. The awareness is partly due to the achievement of political independence by a number of under-developed countries. Partly also it is due to the contact that has been established between different nations of the world through the many international organizations —political, social and economic—that have come into being in recent years. The World War, with all its destructive consequences, has not been altogether purposeless.

The under-developed countries, with their newly acquired political independence, are not only more conscious than ever before of the woeful economic stagnation that they have been through all these years; they are also confident that a breakthrough is possible. In the more advanced countries also there is growing realization that the under-developed regions of the world are an entity to be reckoned with—that what happens in these regions is not altogether outside the realm of their concern and their responsibility.

Now the awareness of the problem is one thing, its solution is another. The need for some kind of a balance in international economic relations (international economic integration, as Myrdal would call it) is great, but the task is enormous. It has been estimated by Dr V. K. R. V. Rao that, on the assumption that under-developed countries have on the average a population growth of 2 per cent per year and an increase in gross national product of 8 per cent per year, they would attain by the year 1974 a standard of living which is less than a fifth of the 1956 level of the Western Hemisphere and about a third of Western Europe. Further, even if these countries have a growth rate of 15 per cent per year for another fifteen years, they will still be at a level just about a tenth of the 1956 level of the United States and Canada and a fourth of the United Kingdom and France.[1] The figures are revealing. And when regard is had to the fact that our under-developed world comprises no less than 70 per cent of the human race, the problem of international economic integration does appear bewildering.

## V

What could be our approach to the problem? There are those who lament the passing away of the age of liberalism, thinking that it is restrictionism in international trade that is responsible for the widening gulf between countries, that the removal of restrictionism is *the* way to international economic balance. The argument has a good deal of validity in so far as the 'world' consists only of the countries of Western Europe. The establishment of the European Free Trade Area and the European Common Market is surely a move in the right direction. But when our world includes, as it does,

[1] V. K. R. V. Rao, *International Aid for Economic Development*, Montagu Burton Lecture, 1960, University of Leeds. (Rough copy with the author.)

the under-developed countries as well, the situation takes on a different complexion. Free trade between unequals, as we have seen, accentuates inequality instead of reducing it.

It may perhaps be argued, however, that the principle of economic liberalism dictates not merely free trade in goods but also free movement of capital and labour. And of course, whatever may be the implications of free trade in goods, movement of factors as such should be a force towards equalizing factor incomes in different countries. If capital flows to where there is scarcity, and labour moves away from where there is abundance of it, tendencies are surely released which make for an approach towards international economic equality. There is no doubt that in some form or other this is the approach that one would recommend. But the approach is not as simple as it appears.

There are serious limitations to mobility of labour. One would surely look askance at the rigid immigration laws operating in the ridiculously sparsely populated areas such as Canada or Australia. There is a strong case for the removal of these laws. But even if these obviously silly restrictions are abolished, there are reasons for doubt as to how far the response from the over-populated areas will be adequate, and, in so far as there is migration from these areas, how far the migrants will find it possible to get integrated into the society of their adoption. Large scale migration, such as is indicated in the context of international economic balance, may indeed create more problems than it solves; even within a country transfer of population from one region to another is by no means an easy problem.

The position of capital is also very much the same. The under-developed countries need capital and would surely welcome it to the extent that their absorptive capacity warrants. But resistance comes from the other side. This is on account of the risk involved in foreign investment. When you invest in your own country you are normally protected by laws and systems over which you have yourself some influence. When you invest it abroad you surrender yourself to the laws and systems belonging to strange and unfamiliar lands. This is why foreign investment has always tended to have some kind of political or military control associated with it. The history of colonialism bears ample testimony to this. Investment, more than trade, has followed the flag. Even apart from this, historically whatever foreign investment the under-developed countries have received has found its way mainly to plantations, oil and other natural resources where profit is high; it has contributed little to the general growth of these economies, which is what is necessary for international balance.

The considerations set out here concerning mobility of labour and capital are perfectly general, and are independent of whether the economies are capitalistic or socialistic. In its dealings with an under-developed country—be they in respect of immigration or in respect of capital exports—a socialist government would not surely behave more favourably than a capitalist one; for all you know it may behave less favourably. Socialism may be—indeed is—an effective instrument of national economic integration; by itself it is as innocuous as any system in respect of international economic integration. To be effective in this latter context, socialism has to be internationalized.

This leads us to the crux of the matter. Not the political structure *within* a State, but *the absence of an international authority, which could deal with individual States in the manner in which an individual State deals with its constituents, is what prevents international economic integration.*

The world State, however, is still a utopia—a 'divine event', as Lord Robbins once put it,[1] towards which the best minds of our diverse civilizations must constantly strive, but which, considering the state of human progress, is not to be realized in any near future. What then remains to be done? No doubt the under-developed countries must raise their rate of growth to the maximum permitted by their resources; help, like charity, must begin at home. It is one of the refreshing features of post-war developments that the under-developed countries have realized the urgency of the task and are going ahead with plans to improve their standard of living. What they have yet to realize is that their bargaining power in the international market is still weak, and that if they are to strengthen it they must 'combine'. They have only to take a lesson from what the trade union movement has achieved by way of national economic integration. In the national sphere we have experienced countervailing balancing processes which can be just copied for application to the international sphere.

But this is not all. If it were, I would perhaps have to conclude with essentially a pessimistic note. For if the under-developed countries were to be left entirely to themselves, it would be a long way before anything approaching international economic integration could be achieved. The resources of these countries are inadequate, their saving capacity small and, each being at a low stage of economic development, they are naturally not generous enough in their relations with one another. What, however, makes one less pessimistic is the institution of International Aid—one of the most significant developments of the post-war era. In their endeavour to accelerate the rate of economic growth, the under-developed countries have the benefit of aid from the more advanced countries of the world. It does look as if aid for economic development is

[1] Lionel Robbins, *Economic Causes of War* (London, 1939), p. 105.

becoming one of the acknowledged principles of public finance in these countries. The volume of aid hitherto received by under-developed countries is of course not adequate, considering the needs of these countries. Nor are all advanced countries equally aware of their responsibility in the matter; the main burden has been taken up by the United States of America. It is also not clear how far the institution of foreign aid is a firm institution based on a genuine sense of international co-operation or how far it is inspired by political exigencies. The cold war renders our vision hazy and makes discrimination a difficult affair. Yet the fact that the system of foreign aid is being gradually institutionalized through the establishment of international agencies does encourage hope.

# 16

# THE RELATION OF FOREIGN AID TO HOME INVESTMENT*

## I

Is the significance of foreign economic aid to be judged simply by the amount of aid or by something more? Can an under-developed economy be self-sufficient in the matter of planned investment for development purposes? If not, what is the degree of dependence that home investment has on foreign resources, and how far is it possible for the planning country to secure the necessary foreign resources without foreign loans or grants?

The matter can conveniently be put in terms of finance. Suppose that the entire finance required for a scheme of public investment is available within the country either by way of internal savings or by way of taxation. Does it necessarily ensure command over the real resources that the scheme involves? If the necessary resources are all available within the country the answer is simple. If, on the other hand, a part of the resources has to be imported, complications crop up, and we have the familiar 'transfer' difficulties. This indeed is one of the things that a purely 'financial' approach to planning seems to ignore. Foreign aid removes these complications by placing foreign resources directly at the disposal of the receiving country. In so far as foreign resources are a necessary complement of domestic resources in a given scheme of economic development, the aggregate home investment that is made possible by foreign aid is a multiple of the amount of the aid. What is the value of this multiplier, and on what does it depend?

## II

Assume that the technical coefficient of the planned investment is fixed, so that the ratio between the foreign constituent and the domestic constituent of the investment plan is also fixed. Assume further that the economy where the additional investments are planned for developmental purposes is otherwise in a state of foreign trade equilibrium, and that beyond the point of equilibrium the elasticity of exports is zero. The foreign aid multiplier can then be readily deduced from the import content of the development plan;

* Originally published in *The Economic Weekly*, Special Number, June, 1955.

for it turns out to be the reciprocal of the ratio of the foreign constituent to the aggregate investment planned. If, for example, this ratio is 1:4—if, in other words, the foreign constituent is 25 per cent of the planned investment, the foreign aid multiplier is 4. If the ratio is 1:5, the foreign aid multiplier is 5. And so on—the value of the multiplier varies inversely with the import content of the investment plan. If, on the other hand, the technical coefficient is freely variable —if, that is to say, the foreign resources can be freely substituted by internal resources, or alternatively, if the elasticity of exports of the country is infinity, the foreign aid multiplier comes down to unity. In this latter case, the benefit that the country derives from foreign aid is just equal to the amount of the aid; if foreign aid is surrendered, aggregate investment is less by just the amount of the aid.

A numerical example will make the matter clear. Suppose that a country plans an investment of the order of Rs 1000 crores, of which the foreign constituent in physical terms is worth Rs 200 crores. The import content is thus 20 per cent of the planned investment. Now, the planning authority, let us say, collects enough savings to finance the internal share of the investment, i.e. Rs 800 crores. On our first assumption, a foreign grant or loan of the balance of Rs 200 crores makes it possible for the country to carry the entire scheme of investment through, while its absence renders the entire scheme abortive. In this case the surrender of foreign aid of the order of Rs 200 crores results in a loss of investment of the order of Rs 1000 crores. On our second assumption, on the other hand, there are two possibilities. In so far as the method of production is freely variable, the investment pattern can be so chosen as to be independent of foreign resources. And in so far as exports are perfectly elastic, one-fifth of the internal savings (i.e. Rs 160 crores) can be used for the purchase of exportable goods within the country against which an equivalent amount of foreign exchange can be secured. In either case the loss of investment due to the surrender of foreign aid turns out to be just Rs 200 crores, the volume of investment being reduced from Rs 1000 crores to Rs 800 crores.

## III

The conclusion deduced from our first assumption is something of a paradox: the value of the foreign aid multiplier is high if the share of the foreign constituent in a piece of investment is relatively low, and vice versa. It thus looks as if the less dependent an under-developed country is on foreign resources for the implementation of its plan, the greater is the significance of foreign aid. But the paradox is more apparent than real. It is true that the conclusion is unavoidable if we follow our assumption strictly; even a small link, if it is weak, mars the strength of an otherwise stout chain. However, the tyranny of complementarity revealed here is tempered by the possibilities of export surplus envisaged in our second set of assumptions; a country can within limits secure command over foreign resources through internal measures. And here obviously the smaller the share of foreign resources in a given plan of investment the greater is the ease with which the necessary export surplus can be created. The point may be illustrated with reference to a few hypothetical cases.

Case A: Import Content 20 per cent

| | | *Rs* (*Crores*) |
|---|---|---|
| (1) | Foreign aid available | 200 |
| | Internally available finance | 800 |
| | Total investment | 1000 |
| (2) | Foreign aid available | *Nil* |
| | Export[1] surplus created ($\frac{1}{5}$ of the internally available finance) | 160 |
| | Total investment | 800 |
| | Loss of investment due to the surrender of foreign aid | 200 |
| | Foreign Aid Multiplier | 1 |
| (3) | Foreign aid available | *Nil* |
| | Export surplus created ($\frac{1}{8}$ of the internally available finance) | 100 |
| | Total Investment | 500 |
| | Loss of investment due to the surrender of foreign aid | 500 |
| | Foreign Aid Multiplier | 2·5 |

Case B: Import Content 40 per cent

| | | *Rs* (*Crores*) |
|---|---|---|
| (1) | Foreign aid available | 400 |
| | Internally available finance | 600 |
| | Total investment | 1000 |
| (2) | Foreign aid available | *Nil* |
| | Export surplus created ($\frac{1}{5}$ of the internally available finance) | 120 |
| | Total investment | 300 |
| | Loss of investment due to the surrender of foreign aid | 700 |
| | Foreign Aid Multiplier | 1·75 |

[1] Export surplus is in value terms and thus takes account of changes in barter terms of trade, if any, that takes place in view of the raising of exports.

| | |
|---|---|
| (3) Foreign aid available | *Nil* |
| Export surplus created | |
| ($\frac{1}{8}$ of the internally available finance) | 75 |
| Total Investment | 187·5 |
| Loss of investment due to the surrender of foreign aid | 812·5 |
| Foreign Aid Multiplier | 2·03 |

## IV

The general assumption in all these cases is one of fixed technical coefficient, i.e. to say, a fixed ratio of foreign exchange requirement to the total investment plan. In Case A the ratio is 1:5, and in Case B the ratio is 1:2·5. And yet, in so far as there are possibilities of the creation of export surplus, the multiplier is so damped down that under certain conditions its value becomes less in Case A than in Case B. In Case A(2) for example, the foreign aid surrendered is Rs 200 crores and the consequent loss of investment is also Rs 200 crores, so that the foreign aid multiplier is unity. In the corresponding case under B, the foreign aid surrendered is Rs 400 crores, and the loss of investment is Rs 700 crores, so that the foreign aid multiplier comes up to 1·75. Cases A(3), B(2) and B(3) are specially interesting. They bring out one significant feature of an under-developed economy, namely that the total realized investment may often fall below the internally available finance. The bottle-neck in these economies is not always finance. Even if adequate finance is available, investment may often lag behind schedule on account of the non-availability of necessary technical resources for which these economies have to depend on foreign sources.

The degree of complementarity of various types of technical resources in any investment plan is a function of the period within which the plan is sought to be realized. The shorter the period the greater is the technical rigidity of the investment components. In the context of rapid economic development, which happens to be the aim of the under-developed countries, the proportion of the foreign exchange requirement to an investment plan is likely to be more or less fixed. In the case of India it is supposed to be around 20 per cent, while in the case of the comparatively less developed economies, it would perhaps be 35–40 per cent. The International Bank, for example, puts the figure at 33·5 per cent for Columbia and at 36 per cent for Ceylon, while Ceylon's own Colombo Plan estimates a figure of 35 to 40 per cent. The conditions in other under-developed economies would not surely warrant a substantially smaller figure. While, however, in India the import content of the development plan is relatively low, in so far as its economy is more diversified, the scope for the creation of export surplus is also relatively large, particularly when account is taken of the flexibility of the policy of import restrictions. The cases considered above, even though hypothetical in character, may therefore serve as a basis for the measure of the foreign aid multiplier in these countries. If Case A approximates to the conditions of India and Case B approximates to the conditions of the relatively less developed economies, then, considering their respective scope for the creation of export surplus, the value of the foreign aid multiplier in these countries would in all probability lie between 1·5 and 2. This is just a guess and should be taken at what a guess is worth; the object of this paper is mainly to indicate the lines on which the gain from foreign aid is to be investigated.

# 17

# FOREIGN BALANCE IN A DEVELOPING ECONOMY*

## I

I start with the definition of a developing economy—a pedestrian start, yet a useful one. The initial position of a so-called developing economy is one of low-level stagnation. The warranted rate of growth, to use Harrod's well-known terminology, is lower than the natural rate of growth, and the actual rate of growth, unlike in the Harrod formula, has no tendency to keep pace with the natural rate. The former happens because the propensity to save is low relatively to the growth of population. And the latter is due to the lack of entrepreneurship in the economy. It is this latter that prevents chronic inflation. You have the spectacle in such an economy of the rate of capital formation lagging behind the growth of population and a state of chronic depression accompanied by growing unemployment. The description fits fairly well the Indian economy as it was till the Second World War. During the war the economy received a jolt through a large foreign investment by way of exports, not accompanied by corresponding imports or internal savings. The result was, thanks to insufficiency of excess capacity in the economy, the notorious inflation of the forties.

Let us, then, revert to the initial position of a developing economy. Let us assume that the initial state is one of balance, both internal and external. Internally savings are equal to investment, and externally imports are equal to exports. There is neither inflation nor deflation, and yet the rate of investment and hence of capital formation is low relatively to the growth of population and there is chronic poverty. The purpose of the present paper is to follow up the impact of a process of rapid economic development of such an economy—it is in this sense that we call it a developing economy—upon its foreign balance.

The process, let us say, is initiated by the state as a matter of policy, seeing that left to itself the economy would not move out of its rut. The State can do this by persuading or forcing the people to save more, thus moving the warranted rate of growth towards the natural rate and itself providing the needed entrepreneurship, so as to keep the actual rate of growth up to the warranted rate. It can

* Originally published in *The Economic Weekly*, Annual Number, February, 1963.

also do this by taking loans or other forms of aid from foreign countries, in which case, for the time being at any rate, the burden of saving is shifted to foreigners.

If the latter alternative is open—and that depends upon the readiness with which foreign countries are prepared to offer aid—the process of economic development gets on smoothly. If the aid comes in the form of loans, there is no doubt the question of amortization. But if we confine ourselves to a period over which foreign loans are continuous and they are also sufficient to take care of amortization, then there is no complication; over the given period the difference between loans and grants fades away.

Difficulties arise when the developing country fails to secure foreign aid and has to depend upon its own resources. Foreign aid serves two purposes. On the one hand it relieves the economy of the burden of extra savings; on the other hand it provides foreign exchange to the economy with which it can import capital goods and know-how essential for rapid economic development. Note that it is in the context of *rapid* economic development that the need for foreign exchange assumes special significance. For after all if the economy can bear slow progress, or is not anxious to avoid excessive costs, internal resources may be enough to give it the necessary push; surely the first country that started economic development did not seek another planet to import capital goods from! The whole question boils down to the degree of substitutability, within a prescribed time limit, between domestic resources and foreign resources: the shorter the time within which a given level of development has to be compressed, the lower is the degree of substitutability. Given the need for additional foreign exchange and given the fact that foreign aid is not available—at any rate not available to an extent adequate for the rate of growth aimed at, the State has to face the task of converting the newly created domestic savings into foreign capital.[1]

Now even here, in so far as the additional savings result in the release of commodities which can be exported at constant terms of trade, there is no trouble. If, on the other hand, exports are not sufficiently elastic, then a part of normal imports of the country is to be converted into capital goods needed for economic development. Here again the process of conversion does not create any hitch if the additional savings are accompanied by a curtailment of normal spending on imports to an extent sufficient to pay for the necessary capital goods. If they are not, then the need for import restrictions arises; the economy faces potentially an adverse foreign balance.

[1] See 'The Relation of Foreign Aid to Home Investment', above.

## II

A smooth transition of an economy from stagnation to progress is thus not inconceivable, particularly when foreign aid supplements the economy's own efforts. But the conditions making for it are much too hypothetical; it is very much more probable that the transition will be marked by an adverse foreign balance which will need to be met by forced restriction of normal imports. It will be the contention of this note that the state of unbalance in foreign trade tends to pursue the economy in the entire course of economic growth, in so far as the rate of growth is maintained or accelerated over a given period. Internal maladjustments of an inflationary character, if these take place, as they often do, only reinforce the tendency. These additional complications, however, are not considered here; the assumption is the extreme-most favourable one of equality between aggregate saving and aggregate investment at constant prices.

With the growth of the economy, will the degree of unfavourableness in foreign balance be growing, remain constant or be reduced? The answer to this obviously depends upon the rate at which exports will be growing relatively to imports. With an initial trade deficit covered by foreign reserve or aid, the degree of unbalance will be reduced only when the rate of growth of exports substantially exceeds the rate of growth of imports. For even if the rate of growth of exports equals the rate of growth of imports, the absolute amount of deficit will tend to grow over time. More so will be the case if the rate of growth of exports falls behind the rate of growth of imports.

Assume that the ratio between foreign capital and domestic output remains constant. Then the rate of growth of imports depends solely upon the marginal propensity of income earners to import. If this happens to be higher than the average propensity, the rate of growth of imports will tend to exceed the rate of growth of aggregate income. Now in the case of a developing economy of the type we are envisaging, this may well be the case. For one thing, as a person's income increases he is inclined to shift to superior goods, and since such goods are yet scarce at home, there may be a tendency to turn to imports. The so-called demonstration effect of economic development is an aspect of this tendency. For another, in the course of economic development—at any rate in the earlier stages—the distribution of income tends to be more unequal, if only because growth results in the emergence of shortages in skill and entrepreneurship in the economy for which abnormally high rewards need to be paid. An enlightened Government does no doubt take measures to prevent this tendency; but experience suggests that the tendency is too strong to be eliminated altogether. There is thus a strong probability that in a developing economy the marginal propensity to import should be an increasing function of income.

What happens to exports? Is there any tendency for the elasticity of exports necessarily to assume a value higher than or equal to the income elasticity of imports? Here one does notice a certain lack of symmetry. For, whereas with growing income at home there is a natural tendency for imports to grow, there is no such natural tendency in the case of exports. The behaviour of exports is determined very largely by forces outside the economy. It is a function of the rate of growth in the rest of the world, the regional distribution of income and the state of international competition—factors which are all external to the economy. If the rate of growth in the rest of the world, particularly in those countries with which our developing economy has special trade ties is less than the rate of growth at home, the elasticity of exports of the economy would tend to be lower than the elasticity of imports.

Further, even if the foreign markets show a favourable growth rate, movements in the pattern of trade and in international competition may be such as to prevent our economy from maintaining its share in world exports. While its own consumers would show a tendency, as their incomes grow, to shift to superior foreign goods, thus raising the country's marginal propensity to import, there is less reason to expect that, with equal rates of growth in the rest of the world, there should be a commensurate growth in the foreign consumers' demand for its own exports, especially those that are of a traditional character. A developing economy may thus find itself in a peculiar predicament of having a *growing* deficit in its balance of trade. And in so far as such deficits cannot be met by foreign aid, it has therefore to continue with the policy of trade controls. The experience of our own country during the last twelve years of planned economic development seems to bear this out, although the difficulties inherent in development may have been enhanced here by internal cost inflation.

## III

Harrod sets up an equation of growth for an open economy thus:[1]

$$G_w C_r = s - b$$

where $G_w$ is the warranted rate of growth, $C_r$ is the required capital coefficient, $s$ the fraction of income saved and $b$ the foreign balance. The equation says that if $C_r$ and $s$ remain constant, the value of $G_w$ varies inversely as $b$, or in other words, the warranted rate of growth of an economy falls as its foreign balance increases. For an advanced economy where the saving propensity is so high that the warranted

[1] R. F. Harrod, *Towards Economic Dynamics* (London, 1948), p. 105.

rate of growth exceeds the natural rate of growth and where a reduction in the warranted rate of growth is called for in the interest of full employment, there is justification, Harrod argues, for the maintenance of a positive foreign balance.

Now, just the opposite happens in the case of a developing economy where the saving propensity is low and the warranted rate of growth lags behind the natural rate. Maintenance of a negative foreign balance in such an economy serves, other things remaining the same, to push up the warranted rate of growth towards the natural rate. To lower the warranted rate of growth down to the level of the natural rate, an advanced economy needs an outsider (a 'third person', to use Rosa Luxemburg's famous phrase) to absorb surplus, while to raise the warranted rate growth up to the level of its natural rate, a developing economy needs an outsider to cover deficit.

This does not mean, however, that a developing economy has necessarily to put up with a growing deficit in foreign balance; it cannot afford to—for the simple reason that it is a good deal more difficult to borrow than to lend. Nor does it mean necessarily that, in the absence of adequate foreign aid, it has to continue with trade controls. Increasing marginal rate of saving, such as is associated with planned economic development, serves two purposes. While it raises the warranted rate of growth, it also tends to reduce the rate of growth of trade deficit, even if it does not eliminate it altogether Further, in the perspective of long term growth one must also count on such adjustments in the investment pattern as would ensure that import substitutes and exports bear an increasing ratio to national output. By raising the ratio of import substitutes to national output we can reduce the foreign capital coefficient and by diversifying exports and raising the ratio of exportables to national output, we make it possible for the economy to maintain the same import coefficient without facing a growing deficit in foreign balance. As to whether one or the other should have a higher weightage in the investment pattern of a developing economy, one must keep an open mind; the question has to be answered by our old guide—The Law of Comparative Costs. This reminder is called for particularly in the context of our own planning. For, a considerable amount of futile controversy has gone on here over this choice—the parties in the dispute often forgetting that the production of import substitutes at higher cost than international price is as much a social cost as subsidy to exports.

# 18

# COMMERCIAL POLICY AND ECONOMIC GROWTH*

## I

It is now perhaps generally accepted that the classical theory of commercial policy based on comparative costs has to be revised basically in the context of economic growth of under-developed countries.

High rate of growth is consistent with free trade policy under very exceptional circumstances. If the country is small in size and is such as cannot feed its population with 'corn' internally produced except at an abnormally high price; if conditions are propitious for the introduction of mechanical devices in manufacturing industries, offering scope to division of labour and economies of production; if foreign competition in respect of the country's growing industry is yet distant, so that the international price of export goods is more a function of international demand than of internal cost; if these favourable circumstances exist, the country gains by adopting a policy of free trade. And it is these circumstances that moulded British policy in the mid-nineteenth century and were the basis of English Classical Political Economy.

In different conditions these principles may not apply. Growth has been stimulated in many other countries, such as the United States or Germany, by a policy of protection rather than of free trade. The famous 'infant industry' argument of Frederick List in favour of protection grew out of a realization that a country cannot effect a transition from the agricultural stage to an industrial stage unless its industries are protected by tariff against foreign competition. The classical assessment of gains from international trade is based on *static* comparative cost conditions; it does not take account of the possibility of *changes* in these conditions that a push towards economic development may entail. A country may have comparative advantage in agriculture under *given* circumstances; and if these circumstances are allowed to persist, the peculiar comparative advantage also persists, resulting in its continued specialization in agriculture. But if steps are taken to shift resources from agriculture to industry, certain developments may take place in the country which alter the entire comparative cost configuration. And it may—indeed it often does—pay the country to take these steps as transition

* Originally published in *International Studies*, Vol. IV, No. 2.

measures, even though during the period of transition, the domestic consumers may have to pay higher prices for goods that are shut out.

Basically it is this Listian principle that has provided inspiration to under-developed countries in their effort towards economic development, although, superimposed upon it, there has been the more recent concept of economic planning. There has been accordingly a switch-over from protection as such to trade and payments regulation. Protection is an over-all measure designed to give encouragement to domestic industries; the allocation of resources within the system is left to private enterprise and is determined by the entrepreneurs' motive of immediate profit rather than of long-run growth of the economy as a whole.

Now, it is true that in an economy where there is an adequate supply of entrepreneurship in the industrial sector which, because of late start, was not allowed to function properly, an over-all measure of protection would lead allocation of resources on to channels which are conducive to economic growth. And this is the assumption on which the protectionist argument is generally based. But there are economies where entrepreneurship itself is lacking, where, therefore, the State has to assume the role of an entrepreneur. In such economies protection by itself may turn out to be an oppressive instrument; by creating monopoly conditions, it may do more harm than good to the economy. Moreover, just those lines of production that would receive stimulus from a policy of protection in view of immediate profitability may not be the lines that would make for a high rate of growth. Suppose, to take an example, the strategy of long-run economic development of a country dictates a bias on investment in heavy industries destined to produce capital goods, and suppose also that these are the industries which, considering existing resources, rank low from the point of view of immediate profitability. A general policy of protection will in these circumstances fail to achieve the objective of growth—for it will divert resources to consumption goods industries which have much less strategic significance from the point of view of long-run growth. If the trade policy of under-developed countries has to be oriented towards economic growth, direct control of imports and exports is indicated rather than just a policy of protection of the Listian variety. Since the creation of surplus for investment is the way to economic growth, a growth-oriented trade policy must aim at creating the maximum possible trade surplus in consumption goods, and then converting the surplus into capital goods which have strategic significance for growth. This necessarily involves a more searching regulation of the pattern of foreign trade than would be secured by a policy of over-all protection.

Let it be noted at once that the policy affects the *pattern* of foreign trade; it does not reduce its volume. On the other hand, the capital requirements of under-developed economies are such that world trade increases in volume in the process of their planned development. Here also there is a vital difference between protection as such and a policy of trade control aimed at economic growth. Protection does tend to reduce the volume of international trade—at any rate in the short run—whereas a growth-oriented trade control policy tends to increase it.

One may perhaps ask at this stage why there should be at all any need for foreign trade control when what is needed is the creation of an over-all investible surplus. When one imports less and exports more, one may be said to 'save'. It is this saving that is converted into capital goods for purposes of economic development. Could not the same purpose be served by domestic savings alone, with exports and imports left free? For realizing the desired rate of savings, could we not operate exclusively on the domestic market and with the surplus thus created secure through trade whatever foreign exchange was needed to give effect to planned growth? This surely would be possible provided the surplus generated through domestic savings could be converted into necessary capital goods at *constant costs*. And this would either require that the import content of planned investment is infinitely flexible or that exports of the planning country are perfectly elastic.

Domestic saving, in financial terms, means withdrawal of a part of income from current expenditure on consumption goods. The effect of such withdrawal is that, at current prices, some of the goods produced are left unsold in the domestic market. The goods thus released must either be transformed internally into capital goods, or else exported in exchange for capital goods produced in foreign countries. Now either of the processes is subject to increasing costs—at any rate, in the short run.[1] Even if the goods released are wage-goods and raw materials which are capable, technologically, of being transformed internally into necessary capital goods, the process of transformation must be time-consuming and the rate of transformation must be higher than the international rate. Internal resources are not perfect substitutes of external resources. Nor is it so easy to get the good exported, specially under the present conditions of international trade and payments. For exports to have the necessary degree of elasticity, there are at least three conditions that must be satisfied: (i) the goods must be in general demand in the international market; (ii) the volume of exports from the country in question must form a very small part of the aggregate international demand for the goods; (iii) the current domestic price of the goods, together with cost of transport and other charges, must not be

[1] See 'The Relation of Foreign Aid to Home Investment', above.

higher than their international price. One has only to look at the nature of the conditions to realize that they are not even approximately fulfilled in the context of rapid economic development such as under-developed countries intend to achieve.

Under-developed countries need to import machinery and other kinds of capital resources from more advanced countries. If they have to produce all these internally, development is bound to become slow and more expensive. On the other hand, if internal savings are to be transformed via exports into external capital, there is bound to be some reaction on the terms of trade. There is indeed a certain degree of rigidity in the import content of investment in developing economies, and the elasticity of exports, particularly to countries which are to supply the necessary capital goods, is certainly less than infinity. All this makes it essential for the under-developed countries to operate on foreign markets for the supply of foreign exchange wherewith to buy capital goods needed for development. The *raison d'être* of foreign trade control lies in this.

## II

One of the major factors determining the economic growth of a country is the rate of capital formation, or in other words, the ratio of investment to income. A high rate of growth of an economy depends, other things remaining the same, upon the maintenance of a high proportion of investment goods in the income structure. Import of capital goods therefore stimulates economic growth only in so far as it helps the maintenance of a high investment ratio in the economy. If, on the other hand, the process that brings capital goods into the economy is also a process that provides incentive to increased consumption within the country, then there is leakage. And to the extent that such leakages take place growth is retarded. This consideration is of the utmost significance for the relation of commercial policy to economic growth. However well-designed a country's commercial policy may be, whatever the external surplus that it succeeds in creating, it goes awry unless the internal production policy is also adjusted to the requirements of growth.

Suppose, for example, an under-developed country decides to restrict the import of luxury and semi-luxury goods in order to acquire foreign exchange for the purchase of plants and machinery to aid economic development. The procedure is a perfectly legitimate one signifying, as it does, just a shift in the consumption pattern of the people over time; and there is nothing in our economic categories to suggest precisely how far such shifts might be permitted, the die-hard free-traders notwithstanding. Now in so far as the internal production structure helps maintain the investment ratio implicit in the external trade policy, the economy secures a higher rate of growth. If on the other hand the shelter of import restrictions is permitted to create industries within the economy producing just those good whose imports are restricted, then the objective of growth is frustrated; the economy surrenders through the back-door what it secures by the front-door.

Perhaps even more. And here the free trade argument based on differences in comparative costs comes into its own. It is one thing to conserve foreign exchange for the import of plant and machinery designed to help economic growth; it is an entirely different thing to use import restrictions as a device for stimulating domestic manufacture of 'protected' goods. Industrialization is not synonymous with economic growth. While a judicious process of industrialization helps economic growth, a wrong process of industrialization retards it. The goods whose imports are restricted with a view to the saving of foreign exchange in the context of growth are not necessarily goods in whose production the economy has a potential advantage. The so-called 'infant industry' argument may not apply to these cases. And in so far as it does not, to use resources for the production of such goods is waste which a developing economy cannot surely afford.[1]

This is simple logic, and yet it is so often ignored. In our own country, for example, while import of luxury goods such as cars, refrigerators, air-conditioners etc., are virtually prohibited, their production is permitted, even though their internal cost will often be more than double the international price. This is waste, and when account is taken of the fact that a considerable proportion of the resources needed for their production consists of imported parts, which involve the use of foreign exchange anyway, the waste comes out particularly conspicuously. In case the supply of these goods is considered urgent at all, economic considerations would justify a straightforward policy of import—preferably of course through State trading, so that the supply may be kept within a prescribed limit and the shortage-induced excess profit may not go into the hands of a few favoured importers. It is true, as one may argue, that in view of the scarcity of foreign exchange higher weightage must be given to foreign resources as against domestic resources in cost calculation in a developing economy. It is surely arguable that the difference between domestic costs and international prices of these goods is partly nominal and that it would narrow down to the extent that saving of foreign exchange is given higher weightage. Yet on any reasonable assumption concerning the relative weight of

[1] See I. G. Patel, 'Trade and Payments Policy for a Developing Economy,' *International Trade Theory in a Developing World*, ed. Roy Harrod (London, 1963), pp. 319–20.

foreign and domestic resources it would appear that the domestic production of most of the luxury goods in an under-developed economy is wasteful even if the growth criterion is waived. If, for example, the cost of an 'Ambassador' car produced in India is twice as high as the price of an imported car of comparable quality, and if the domestic car is manufactured *entirely* out of domestic resources, then its production has economic justification only so long as a rupee-worth of external resources is considered at least twice as important as a rupee-worth of domestic resources. In the more realistic case where a part of the cost of domestic production consists of expenditure on imported materials, the weight given to external resources has to be higher still if domestic production is to be justified in economic terms. Domestic production of luxury and semi-luxury goods that flourishes under the shelter of import restriction is not only inimical to growth, it is also in most cases uneconomical, judged by the criterion of current income maximization.

## III

We have seen that commercial policy in a developing economy must be directed to the realization, through export surplus on current consumption account, of enough foreign exchange to feed the process of investment involved in the planned target of growth. The process is no doubt eased by foreign aid and, thanks to the growing awareness in the advanced countries of the need for international economic co-operation, foreign aid is becoming a significant element in the financing of economic development of under-developed countries. Yet foreign aid, even as it is, covers only a part of external finance in the context of rapid economic development of these countries; the remaining part must necessarily be export surplus on current account.

Now a country can create export surplus by cutting down imports and by increasing exports. If adequate foreign exchange is to be secured to give effect to a development plan involving the use of imported capital goods, imports of consumption goods must be cut down below the normal level and exports must be pushed up beyond the normal level. A rational commercial policy must have both these methods in view. Whereas, however, the decision to import less is a one-party decision, the decision to export more involves two parties—the country sending exports and the country receiving them. This is why under-developed countries are often bound to place more reliance on import restriction than on export promotion in their endeavour to secure foreign exchange for developmental purposes.

It is indeed mainly through curtailment of imports that the foreign exchange requirements of a development plan have to be met—at any rate in the early stages of planning in an under-developed country. And in most of the under-developed countries there is a fairly good scope for such curtailment. It is one of the evil paradoxes of an under-developed country that while the vast majority of the population is subnormally poor, there is a section which earns enough to enable it to indulge in imported luxuries. Controls may conveniently be applied, as they are being applied in the developing countries, to these imports. For luxury goods are, by definition, goods shortage of which does not affect the productive efficiency of the people. They are non-essentials from the point of view of economic growth and one can extend the list of such goods according to one's conception of the degree of non-essentiality. How far controls on such imports can be carried and what impression they would produce on balance of trade in any specific case depends, first, upon the significance of luxury items in the normal import basket of the country and, secondly, upon the political pull of its so-called U-sector.

While there should not be much disagreement concerning the nature of import items to be subjected to control in the context of planned development, there may be differences concerning the method of control to be adopted. Broadly there are three alternative methods of import control—tariff, quotas and State trading, and all these are practised in varying degrees by the developing countries. Choice between these methods is not always a matter of abstract principle; it is conditioned by the social and political environment of a country and also by the degree of efficiency of its administrative machinery. Tariff surely is a method which is least offensive to the liberal principle and, provided it is adjusted properly, it is also a method which prevents the emergence of excess profit in the market for imported goods. But its effectiveness is uncertain. What is that system of tariff which in our own country, for example, would prevent the inflow of luxury goods such as cars, refrigerators or air-conditioners beyond what would be warranted by the degree of foreign exchange scarcity relatively to the plan? Even the present 150 per cent duty on cars would surely be too low for the purpose if it were not supplemented by direct control. On the other hand, the quota system based on licenses to 'approved dealers', though apparently effective in limiting imports to a prescribed level, is discriminatory, and it leads to all kinds of corruption—in actual practice, often frustrating the very purpose for which it is supposed to stand. Cases of surreptitious dealings are not uncommon in our own country, as reports go, and the situation must be the same in other countries as well where the quota system is in operation.

It is often suggested that licences should be auctioned to highest bidders, so that the difference between the internal market price of the imported goods and its landed price might be reduced to a minimum. The device seems commendable and, although it smacks of the much maligned system of multiple exchange rates, there is no reason why the IMF or the GATT should not permit it, having regard to the peculiar circumstances of a developing economy. After all it is only a refinement of the quota system, meant for internal cost-price adjustment; it does not open up new avenues of discrimination. Indeed it amounts to a combination of the quota system with high tariff, with this difference that whereas the level of tariff is fixed by the state and cannot be readily adjusted to the market situation, the price of an auctioned import licence is fixed by competitive dealers and is dictated by market forces.

At the same time the policy of auctioning licences under a quota system is not essentially different from State trading. Both operate within a prescribed quota, and in both the excess of the internal market price over the landed price of the imported goods is appropriated by the State. Unless, therefore, the State not only prescribes the quota but also wishes to control the internal market price of the relevant goods, the difference between the two systems turns out to be one of form. In the one case the State takes the margin from traders buying import licence, in the other it is recovered from the ultimate buyers of imported goods.

It thus appears that a rational commercial policy whose aim is to cut down imports to a planned minimum has to choose between the quota system supplemented by high tariff or licence auctioning on the one hand and the system of State trading on the other. Given a firm approach, the end can be achieved by either of these methods. In a democratic society, however, where public opinion does not view nationalization with favour and specially where established traders have some political pull, the preference obviously will be for the former. On the other hand, if the quota system leads to conspicuous abuse and corruption, the Government may, even if reluctantly, be driven to adopting the policy of State trading Whatever the method, import restriction is to operate as the chief instrument for meeting the foreign exchange gap associated with planned economic development in its initial stages.

Export promotion is by far a more difficult job for an under-developed country, specially in the short run. Indeed one of the characteristics of an under-developed economy is absence of variety, and hence of resilience, in exports. These countries have generally a set pattern of exports, commodity-wise as well as country-wise. They cannot easily make shifts in the pattern; introduction of new varieties of exports and cultivation of new markets take time and are themselves largely dependent on the level of economic development that a country has already attained. The difficulty is enhanced by the fact that a process of planned development is almost invariably accompanied by a rise in prices and costs in the economy. 'Development with stability' is a counsel of perfection which it is difficult for a developing economy to conform to—if only in view of the pressure that rapid growth brings to bear on the labour market.

Export subsidies, excise duties with rebates on exports, retention quotas etc., are the usual devices for export promotion. These devices are however uncertain in their effect on exports, in so far as they are applied to the current flow of goods and the current pattern of production; the traditional exports of these countries are not elastic enough. If an attack is made on all fronts, some result may perhaps be achieved; but considering the possible yield from such measures and considering also their implications for terms of trade, one wonders if they are worthwhile. The futility of such measures is amply illustrated by the experience of our own country. With all the export promotion schemes that the country has had, its export during the first ten years of planning remained more or less stagnant, although world export trade doubled and its own income increased by 42 per cent. Those who in the face of these facts, talk glibly about export promotion in our country and expect by just short-term devices to secure an annual increase of 15–16 per cent in our exports in the course the Third Five Year Plan do not seem to know what they are talking.

All this does not suggest relegating exports into any minor role in the context of economic growth. Far from that. In some countries development of export trade may be *the* limiting factor of economic growth. It is, however, in the long-term perspective that exports emerge as an important factor of economic growth. What must be the investment pattern, what proportion of aggregate resources and what kinds of resources must be devoted to exportables, considering other possibilities, in order that enough foreign exchange can be earned, as plans proceed, to sustain a prescribed rate of growth—these are the relevant questions to be asked in that context. The choice in this perspective will be between goods that have export potential and goods that can substitute imports; import restrictions as such must necessarily assume an increasingly minor role, as plans proceed. Indeed economic development would lose all significance if import restrictions of any sort were to remain a long-term feature of an economy.

In choosing the current investment pattern with a view to a future flow of foreign exchange—for this is what a long-term perspective implies—one must, however, invoke the principle of comparative costs again. It would be absurd in this context not to keep clear of any philosophy favouring either import substitutes or exports; the criterion must be the economic criterion of long-run comparative costs. Foreign trade is not an isolated phenomenon. It must be considered as an integral part of a development plan. The aim of commercial policy must be to help this long-term process of growth as much as it is to solve the immediate problem of foreign exchange that an economy may face at a particular stage. Indeed the latter problem will be the less acute the more earnestly attention is given to the former.

*Part IV*

# TEACHING ECONOMICS

# 19

# THE TEACHING OF ECONOMICS*

## I

There has been some heart-searching in recent years concerning the manner in which Economics should be taught in universities—the period over which teaching should be extended, the courses that it should cover, the level at which it should be imparted, and so on. Teaching of Economics has been the subject of two successive Presidential Addresses to the Royal Economic Society.[1] More recently Mrs Robinson gave vent to a sense of frustration at the kind of economics that is taught at Cambridge.[2] While Lord Robbins and Sir Alexander Carr-Saunders had a local audience in view when they delivered their Presidential Addresses, Mrs Robinson's special reference was to the students from India and Pakistan who, she thinks, have been taking more eagerly to economic studies these years than their British counterparts.

While Mrs Robinson's assessment of our boys is encouraging, and while her anxiety to adjust the teaching of Economics to suit the circumstances of our society deserves our appreciation, one feels depressed when one reflects upon the way the matter is being handled at our end. How are our own universities behaving? What awareness do they have of the increasing importance that Economics as a branch of knowledge is assuming in the country these days? After all only a handful of our students can afford to go over to foreign universities for their education. The bulk of our boys have to be trained here in our own universities. What deficiencies does one notice in the standard of teaching in Economics here, and what steps would one suggest to improve it? It is time we thought seriously about these matters.

Two things are clear. The public in this country, as elsewhere, are placing much greater weight upon Economics and economists than they used to do, say, twenty-five years ago. This is particularly due to the advent of Planning as a means of economic development.

* Originally published in *The Economic Weekly*, Annual Number, February, 1961.

[1] Lionel Robbins, 'The Teaching of Economics in Schools and Universities', *The Economic Journal*, December, 1955; Sir Alexander Carr-Saunders, 'The Place of Economics and Allied Subjects in the Curriculum', *The Economic Journal*, September, 1958.

[2] Joan Robinson, 'Teaching Economics', *The Economic Weekly*, Annual Number, 1960.

There is an increasing awareness of the limitations of the old *laissez faire* principle and the need for conscious control of economic affairs, not merely in the field of distribution but also in the field of consumption and production. Secondly, in view of the growing importance of the subject, a larger proportion of the better type of students are now going in for the Economics course than used to be the case before. In most of our university centres there is clear evidence of a shift away from Philosophy and Literature to Economics; other social sciences are yet not popular enough. Responsibilities of the Economics Faculties in our universities therefore are unquestionably great.

## II

Let me say at once that my special interest is in the teaching of Economics *at the university level.* I would plead, as Lord Robbins does, that Economics is for grown-ups to learn, and I would leave out the subject altogether from the pre-university course. Even at the university, since we have two degrees, unlike London or Cambridge where there is only one, I would concentrate more on the second degree, i.e. MA; for it is there that I would have specialization. At the undergraduate level, Economics is necessarily to be taught along with other subjects, and even though it may be opted for as a major, the kind of training that is expected is necessarily of a general character. The object here would be to provide students with a general knowledge of the various types of economy and the basic tools of economic analysis. Acquaintance with standard texts on the major branches of Economic science together with a dose of Economic history and an appreciation of the course of development of the Indian economy would be enough at this stage. For some this will be part of a system of liberal education which will stand them in good stead in any walk of life they might choose; for others—the would-be specialists—it will be a preparation for undergoing the later specialized course. For the first type of teaching, the universities need faithful teachers; it does not matter if they are just pedestrian.

Much more care has to be taken for the teaching of Economics at the postgraduate level. And it is at this level, I suspect, that we are failing miserably. Anybody who has an eye to see and who has had occasion to examine postgraduate answer-papers in Economics of our universities or to interview candidates for jobs requiring special competence in Economics will have felt that something is frightfully wrong about the teaching of Economics at the postgraduate level. It is no accident that some of our best boys go out to foreign universities for the study of Economics just after their graduation here.

Is there anything wrong about our syllabus? Do we, or do we not teach the right kind of things in our Economics courses? This is the sort of question that Lord Robbins and Sir Alexander Carr-Saunders ask in general and Mrs Robinson asks in the special context of overseas students. I would not argue that we have a perfect syllabus in our universities. Far from that. There is a lot that can be done to improve the content of our postgraduate course. In particular I have a feeling that teaching of Economics, as it is at present in most of our universities, is problem-oriented and not, as it should be, principle-oriented. I have had many quarrels with my colleagues as also with the authorities on this score in the past, and I still do not see why, given the limited time at our disposal, we should not emphasize principles rather than specific problems. There is no end of problems—national and international, and it is only a tiny fraction that you can do justice to, if you take problems for your analysis in the classroom. On the other hand, if you take the boys through 'principles' and bring in problems only as illustrations, you give the boys basic knowledge which they can apply to the analysis of any problem that may come their way as they take up the specialist's jobs. The coverage under 'principles' must, however, be wide; not only 'pure theory', including the theory of growth, but also Money, International Trade, Public Finance, Industrial Organization, etc. have to be there in the syllabus. Considering the advance that has taken place in each of these fields, one may be sure that mere 'principles' would be enough to occupy even the most serious of our students over a period of two years.

Decision as to what to teach and how to teach should not be very difficult to make. We can refer the matter to a body of experts, and I am pretty sure that they can come to an agreed solution. My own view is clear on the matter. Teaching at the postgraduate level should be directed more to tools of analysis than to the enumeration of problems. The efficacy of this method can be gauged from the fact that most, perhaps all, of those who are now handling the concrete problems of our country as Economic Advisers to the Government have had their training in foreign universities whose syllabi contain hardly any reference to problems relating specifically to India. Concrete problems have to be analysed in the light of 'principles' and if you know the latter, you can do the former.

This does not mean that academic teaching should be devoid of content. Not at all. Good economics has never tolerated 'empty economic boxes'. Principles are derived from practice, and it will be a bad day for economic studies if the age-old procedure of linking 'theory' with 'reality' is not followed. While our syllabus should be constructed with a bias on 'principles'—at every stage these principles must be illustrated by events and problems which they reflect, and as far as possible these illustrations should be chosen from Indian experience, historical and current. I would indeed go further to suggest that in the present context of economic teaching and economic practice, it would be extremely helpful if we could devise some means of introducing a two-way traffic between the universities and the Government. It would be a good thing if young Lecturers and Readers were to serve a period occasionally at the offices of our Economic Advisers and officers in the economic service were to have occasional trips to the universities. University dons would then acquire a better feel of economic reality and the hard-pressed economic officers would acquire a wider perspective for judging the nature of reality. I would commend this idea to the consideration of our universities and our Governments—Central and State.

## III

The real problem does not lie in choosing a syllabus or in deciding upon the period of study. The real problem lies in choosing personnel. Who are the persons to whom we would entrust the responsibility of postgraduate teaching? Do we have an adequate number of well-equipped teachers to feed so many universities? There are no less than forty-five universities in our country today.[1] Considering the number of university-going population, the number surely is not too large. Yet, when account is taken of the fact that a number of our more competent economists are attracted away from the university to Government and private firms, I am sure that the number of economists in the country competent to teach Economics at the postgraduate level falls far short of what we need. Assuming that there are eight papers to be taught in MA—taking optional groups, usually the total comes to more than eight papers—we require at least four teachers for each postgraduate department. Altogether, therefore, there is need for wellnigh 200 teachers, preferably at the level of Professors and Readers. Do we have them? The answer is clearly in the negative. The position is made more hopeless by the fact that universities have often a knack of choosing the wrong kind of men as teachers—partly, no doubt, on account of wrong judgement, but partly also on account of parochialism and favouritism.

Now this is a vicious circle. Incompetence breeds incompetence, and the result is a cumulative tendency to depression of standards. This, I suggest, is what is happening in some of our universities, in spite of (or, shall I say, *because of*) our Economics Faculties turning out so many Ph.D.'s and D.Lit.'s every year. In fact I shall not be

[1] The number has since gone up to fifty-five. See Reflections on Higher Education in India in the Light of the Robbins Report, below.

surprised if one discovers a correlation between the rate of growth of doctorates in our Economics Faculties and the fall in the standard of understanding of Economics among the general body of our students.

I feel convinced that it is a dangerous policy to let things alone. The University Grants Commission has a responsibility in this business, and the sooner it wakes up to the absurdities of the situation the better for the future of Economics teaching, probably teaching in general, in our country. I am inclined to suggest that every university centre should not be permitted in the present circumstances to maintain postgraduate teaching in Economics. We may have just about half a dozen centres for the purpose, and let the other centres limit their teaching responsibilities to the BA standard. The number of scholars to be permitted to take up postgraduate studies will have accordingly to be restricted. And where promising students find it difficult to come to these chosen centres, subsidies should be granted to them; payment of subsidy to deserving students may turn out to be a cheaper proposition than maintaining a postgraduate department in each university centre.

Once this course is decided upon, it should not be difficult to choose our centres. The choice may be based upon two considerations; the tradition that a centre has already created and the attraction that it has for such competent economists as would be available for university teaching.

This surely is a drastic suggestion to offer. And yet I do not know how we can escape thinking along this line.

# 20

# THE ECONOMIC ADVISER*

## I

The Economic Adviser is a recent institution. It is just in the post-war period that economists have been coming out in increasing numbers in the role of professional and paid advisers to governments. Not that the older economists did not 'advise'; they did. In fact the entire system of what is known as 'classical political economy' grew around practical issues, and the generalizations that it carried were specially designed to offer prescriptions of policy. Adam Smith was an advocate of free trade, Ricardo of monetary discipline and Malthus of population control. However, to 'advise' was with them a sort of passion, not profession. They deduced economic generalizations and in the light of these generalizations examined the pressing problems of the day. They also saw to it that the generalizations suggested criteria for the behaviour of the State in relation to society.

Gradually with the emergence of the Neo-classical School, economic theory was shorn of its political bias and it took on the character of a science. Economic theory became just an instrument of explanation and ceased to be an engine for the designing of policy. *Political Economy* was buried and we got *Economics* instead. By and large economists became disinterested analysts, bound by the self-imposed restriction arising from their acceptance of the philosophy of neutrality towards ends.[1] Comparative stability in the economy of the West and a spirit of complacence born out of political impotence in the East encouraged this attitude of economists.

Circumstances have changed. The great fluctuations of trade and industry that characterized the economies of the West during the inter-war period, the total war and its economic implications, the post-war dislocations, political independence in the post-war period of a number of countries in the East, a growing awareness in these countries that poverty and economic stagnation are not a necessary evil—all these have brought the economists and the public again closer together.

While economists are becoming more alive to their responsibilities to the society, the society is also paying increasing attention to what the economist has to say on matters of policy. In the process econ-

* Originally published in *The Economic Weekly*, Special Number, July, 1961.

[1] See, however, pp. 22-23, above.

omic theory itself is becoming more operational in character, and the economist is assuming more and more the role of a technician.

The Economic Adviser is an indispensable appendage to State administration nowadays, thanks particularly to the rapid expansion of economic activities in the public sector. In our own country, we have an Economic Adviser with a fairly big staff attached to most of the more important Ministries of the Union Government, besides a whole directorate of economic research associated with the Reserve Bank of India. The result is that whereas previously the economist, even when urged on to prescribe policy, would fix their eyes on broad problems of the society, today our official Economic Adviser is called upon to attend to details; you never know what sort of question your Minister will ask you to answer! Questions may range from whether a particular industry should be in the public sector or the private sector to what, in a given set of circumstances, should be the quantitative relation between the deposit rate and the loan rate of interest of banks, or perhaps to even more minute aspects of the economy.

## II

The task of the Economic Adviser is a difficult one and calls for the highest effort that a social scientist is capable of. No doubt he has to be a good economic theorist and must possess the necessary technical equipment to know the possible interrelations between economic forces. To take a decision on a particular policy you must know how and in what various directions it will produce its effects, and economic theory, if anything, is an analytical way of showing that.

Theory provides to the economist an insight—and its cultivation makes this insight keener—into the variables on which a particular determinant operates, so that when an action is contemplated in the economic field, the economic theorist should be able at once to see the manner in which it is expected to work itself out and the range of phenomena which it is likely to affect. Theory, however, has to be supplemented by judgement and intuition. In matters of policy it rarely happens that argument is wholly on one side. And since empirical facts as they are available in our society are very often unprecise and since quantitative comparisons of alternative situations are not always possible, you have to rely pretty extensively on judgement and intuition for sorting out the more significant aspects of a problem. Your economist must have that 'amalgam of logic and intuition' which Keynes speaks of as essential 'for economic interpretation in its highest form.'[1]

[1] J. M. Keynes, Alfred Marshall, 1842–1924, *Memorials of Alfred Marshall*, edited by A. C. Pigou (London, 1925), p. 25 n.

Nor is this all. The Economic Adviser, if he is to be useful to society has to be more than an economist. It is not enough for him to draw economic conclusions from given data; he has to know how data themselves would be affected by a policy measure. And since a large part of these data concern human beings, the whole range of subjects dealing with human activity and human motivation, such as group psychology, politics and administration come within his jurisdiction. The 'borderlands' of Economics can perhaps be eschewed by the academic economist. But if the economic practitioner neglects these disciplines he does it at society's peril.

Not only that. The Economic Adviser must have intimate acquaintance with the structure and organization of the economy into which he is required to project his ideas. The practising economist has to know his own people and his own environment intimately and not merely from reports, in order fruitfully to apply his scientific knowledge. In a country like India, for example, the Economic Adviser will be well-advised to take occasional trips to villages where the majority of his countrymen live—to have a direct acquaintance with these men on whose thoughts and motivations the success of a policy measure so largely depends. The 'outward' movements such as our advisers so often indulge in these days have to be tempered a little in favour of the more arduous 'inward' movement!

Above all our Economic Adviser must have a disinterested personality. Perhaps this is the most difficult part of his mental training, and yet this is an essential part. For nothing is more inimical to social stability than corruption of any kind on the part of the policy maker. Adam Smith warned his government against relying in matters of economic policy on the advice of the capitalist class on the ground that their interest is antisocial and they are apt to mislead the policy maker. 'The proposal of any new law or regulation of commerce which comes from this order (the capitalists) ought always to be listened to with great precaution, and ought never to be adopted till after having been long and carefully examined, not only with the most scrupulous, but with the most suspicious attention.'[1] The same warning seems to apply to the *middle class* today, and your Economic Adviser is generally recruited from this class. In the discharge of his official duty the adviser must not identify himself with any *class* and must weigh a measure from the broader social point of view.

## III

It is surely a tall demand that we are making of our Economic

[1] Adam Smith, *Wealth of Nations* (Everyman's Edition, Vol. I, p. 232).

Adviser. But considering the responsibilities that he is supposed to bear, these virtues are essential.

And these virtues have also their reward for the man possessing them. For if our practising economist is deprived of the privilege of building models and refining techniques in the analytical field, such as his academic counterpart enjoys, he can take inspiration from the fact that he has a direct hand in moulding the affairs of the society.

In what way does he have to operate in practice, if he is to be effective? The answer cannot be clearcut, for very much depends upon the mutual relation between the person giving advice and the person receiving it. In a way the situation is paradoxical; after all the Economic Adviser is there to satisfy the Minister, and his existence depends in a large measure upon the favour or frown of the Minister. What is worse, as our organization stands today, the Economic Adviser may often be subservient to the Secretariat, too. Where there is conflict, therefore, he is apt to take an easy line by just showing the *pros* and *cons* of a given measure, and reducing his task to putting whatever decision the ruling authority would take in a more precise and elegant form than the latter could ever do. This way lies frustration of the purpose for which the institution of Economic Adviser is supposed to stand.

Your Economic Adviser must be firm in his prescription of policy. His intellectual training and wide knowledge of facts should entitle him to leadership in the formulation of economic policy. It is not enough for him to suggest 'means to attain *given* ends'. He must not shirk the responsibility of choosing ends, too. He is not merely to diagnose; he has also to prescribe. And once he fixes his mind on a particular prescription of policy, he should have the boldness to push it through. If one has the courage of conviction, one can perhaps find ways of getting things done. If you fail to convince your Minister once, you repeat it and go on doing it until even the most recalcitrant Minister comes round to your view, if only for the sake of an experiment.

Here at last we come to the obligations of the party receiving advice. If the Economic Adviser is to function properly, he must be made to feel free to exercise his judgement. The minimum objective condition for this is that he must be independent of and not be a part of the Secretariat. Both the Secretariat and the Adviser would benefit from this separation. And once this was done, the effectiveness of the Economic Adviser would depend upon the manner in which he is used by the Minister. In view of the large area of responsibility that the Modern State is taking in the economic field, the welfare of the society depends very largely on the able guidance of the trained economist whose services are requisitioned for the purpose. The Adviser must therefore be spared enough leisure and opportunity to think patiently on broad policy matters, instead of being dragged into the daily routine work of the Ministry. Briefing the Minister on economic matters is no doubt one of his jobs in a Parliamentary system of Government. But the Minister must know the limit where the Economic Adviser's duty ends. The Economic Adviser is a new institution—yet in its experimental stage; it requires delicate handling if it is not to degenerate into a mere Department of the State.

# 21

# OVER-FULL EMPLOYMENT IN THE ECONOMISTS' SECTOR*

## I

If Keynes gave a concept of involuntary unemployment, it is to Bertil Ohlin that we owe the concept of over-full employment. Both Keynes and Ohlin are interested in maintaining a high level of employment which, for brevity's sake, they call 'full employment'. But Keynes, writing in the mid-thirties, was oppressed by chronic unemployment and the fear of stagnation resulting from a deficiency of effective demand; whereas Ohlin, writing in the late forties, was concerned with the contrary possibility of excessive demand leading an economy off the stage of full employment. The difference in emphasis is explained by the difference in the contemporary situations; the former is a reflection of the depression of the thirties and the latter a reflection of the post-war boom.

While, however, the concept of involuntary unemployment has found its legitimate place in the corpus of economic theory and policy, over-full employment, in spite of its relevance to present-day conditions, has not had an impact on our thinking and policy-making to the extent that it deserves. The reason is not perhaps difficult to find. As an analytical tool, the concept of over-full employment does not have the sharpness that the concept of involuntary unemployment has. It is not at all difficult to see how, in a wage economy, a labourer may not get employment even though he is willing to work at the current rate of wages. But since, in a democratic society at any rate, you do not force a labourer to work, he can surely refuse employment if he chooses. While, therefore, unemployment is not only a possibility but an observed phenomenon, over-full employment appears to be a contradiction in terms. From the policy point of view, too, the former tends to assume greater importance than the latter; we feel more embarrassed at the sight of unemployment than at the sight of labour shortage. The phenomenon of over-full employment thus tends to get merged into one of inflation. And when this latter is associated with a developing economy, we just resign ourselves complacently to what is 'inevitable'. For, are not—so we argue—inflation and resulting bottle-

* Originally published in *The Economic Weekly*, Annual Number, February, 1962.

necks a kind of price that we must pay for rapid economic development?

Yet the waste due to over-employment, even though concealed, is no less sure and no less significant than the waste due to unemployment. Nor should over-employment be identified with inflation as such; for the two are not the same, even though one accompanies the other. Inflation leads to misdirection of resources and thereby impairs the over-all productive efficiency of the economy. Over-employment does more than that; it tends to reduce the efficiency of the labourer by weakening his urge to work. It is with this latter phenomenon that I shall concern myself. For I feel that we in this country are having a state of over-full employment in certain sectors, though not in the economy as a whole. Indeed while our economy still presents a spectacle of serious unemployment and under-employment, one may pick out individual sectors where over-employment seems to have reached a danger-point.

Nowhere perhaps is this phenomenon more conspicuous than in the market for technicians and economists. Whereas, however, the association of technicians with development planning is of a tangible character and the need for their services is more or less determinate, the economists' contribution is not so. There is thus a risk of the demand for economists being exaggerated, particularly when account is taken of the greater political influence of economists *vis-à-vis* the technicians and of the generous grants that 'economic research' has been receiving in recent years from various agencies, internal and external.

Let me not be misunderstood by my fellow-economists. Let them not think that I am a deserter; for I am not. I would not belittle my own profession and, like the proverbial fool, cut off just that branch of the tree on which I am standing. Far from that. I would surely rejoice at the improved position that economics, as a branch of knowledge, has assumed in the country and would surely welcome the boom in the market for our services, provided I were convinced that it did genuine good to the study of economics. It is there that I have my misgivings. For I believe that over-full employment, whether it is global or sectoral, tends to spoil the quality of output, even if it does not reduce its quantity.

## II

Over-full employment, let us remember, is a state of affairs in which there are more vacant jobs than there are people looking for and, one may add, competent to take up these jobs. The state of over-full employment is due to an excessive demand for labour. Its implications for an individual sector are very much similar to those for the economy as a whole, in so far as the sector in question is at all 'specific'—in so far that is, as an increase in its supply involves a fairly long-term process of investment.

First, over-full employment leads to bottle-necks; and the greater the pressure of demand the more serious these bottle-necks turn out to be. The result is that, on the one hand, fresh recruitment is made from among incompetents and, on the other hand, superannuated people are permitted to hold on to their jobs. Now, when this happens, not only does the average output fall but there is also a possibility that the total output should tend to fall, too; when an organization has relatively less efficient persons at both ends, it is not surprising if the middle group also gets spoiled. We have here an instance of what may be called 'external *dis*economies'. Attempts are of course made in such cases to increase the supply of trained personnel. Training courses are opened and sometimes Seminars are arranged for the spread of education in the special field. But then insufficient attention is given to quality. I know of an interesting case which happened sometime during the last war. A certain State (then Provincial) Government in our country found itself in urgent need of agricultural experts who were to help in the improvement of agricultural methods in the region. It therefore issued instructions to an Agricultural College run under its auspices to the effect that the course of training in the College should be reduced from a period of four years, as it originally was, to a period of three years. It was done, but within less than a year the College received fresh instructions reducing the course still further, until in the end, when matters became desperate, the period was reduced to one year. If this could happen in a technical field, how much more is it likely to happen in the field of economics!

Secondly, under over-full employment there is a tendency to excessive turn-over of labour. Such empirical studies as have been made in other countries in this respect suggest that there is an inverse correlation between labour turnover and the volume of unemployment in an occupation. Now, so long as unemployment exists, a little increase in turnover in the course of a process of reduction of unemployment is surely welcome; one is an offset against the other from the productive point of view. But in a state of over-full employment, high labour turnover is a distinct waste. Capricious movements of workers from one job to another reduces the efficiency of an organization not only by reducing the output of the migrating workers, but also by impairing the effectiveness of others whose services are complementary to the former. I am quite sure that one would, if one did some investigation, find serious cases of disturbance of this kind taking place in organizations which employ economists in our country. I have indeed heard of complaints of this character coming not only from private institutions but also from Government Departments. Promotions in these services have become so rapid that the employer finds it extremely difficult to retain people long enough for them to be of real use to him.

Thirdly, it becomes difficult in a state of over-full employment to get the right kind of people at the right time and at right places. There is a tendency to concentration of workers in a few charmed centres, while others may find it difficult to meet even their minimum requirements. Waiting list of buyers is also a common experience in situations of this sort. Ohlin tells us the story of a Russian lady who, during the war, tried to persuade a plumber to repair a small leakage and to see that she did not have to wait as long as three weeks for the job to be done. Similar instances can be cited in respect of appointments of economists in our institutions, with only this difference that here the waiting period runs in terms of months and years and not in terms of weeks.

Finally—and this is not the least important—when jobs are around, workers are apt to pay less regard to discipline. In situations of this kind, it is the employer, rather than the employee, who has to be apologetic when it comes to getting something done outside routine work. I would, on no account, demand subservience on the part of labour of any kind, nor would brook any tyranny on the part of the employer. I do recognize that the assurance of alternative jobs is a protection to the worker against possible maltreatment by his employer. But preservation of the dignity of labour is one thing, indiscipline is another, and I doubt very much that, to ensure the former, we need so precarious a course as *over*-full employment.

## III

What does all this amount to in terms of policy? We have argued that over-full employment is accompanied by bottle-necks, that it leads to excessive turnover, that it makes it difficult for the employer to choose the right kind of personnel at the right time, and finally that it tends to create an environment in which the workers are apt to lose a correct sense of proportion. All this is damaging to the efficiency of a productive organization. We have also argued that on all accounts it appears that the market for economists' services in the country is currently having a state of over-full-employment, thanks to the urgency created by the plans for economic development, continuance of which, one is afraid, might do damage to the economists' profession as such. For after all, if we are to be true to ourselves, we must tell the society how best to allocate our scarce resources; we economists, of all persons, cannot afford to neglect the problem of allocation of funds.

Does this mean that economists are asked to pass a self-denying ordinance and cut down their demand for funds? Is it by curtailing *demand* that shortages in the market for their services are to be relieved? That by no means is the only approach that our analysis leads to; nor is it a desirable approach, when regard is had to the future of economic studies in the country. There is the altnerative approach calling for an increase in the *supply* of economists, and it is this that I would plead for. *Intra*-sectoral, not *inter*-sectoral, re-allocation of resources is what I would urge for the solution of our problem. I would surely accept whatever grants we may for the extension of economic studies in the country. Having accepted them, however, I would consider more carefully than is being done at the moment how best to use these grants within our own sphere of activity. As it is too much of emphasis is given to 'research'. And in so far as a large share of whatever supply of competent economists we have is drawn away by Research Institutions and Government Departments, 'teaching' suffers and the source from which further supply should be forthcoming is weakened. This surely is an unsatisfactory situation. Matters are made worse by the fact that many of our University Economics Departments, whose main concern must be to 'teach', are gradually being converted into miniature Research Institutions, thanks to the generous grants that they are receiving from the Research Programmes Committee of the Planning Commission.

It is time we shifted our emphasis a little from so-called research to actual teaching, strengthened certain centres of economic studies which have had a tradition and introduced a liberal system of scholarships to enable deserving students to come over to our stronger centres for postgraduate studies. We need to produce more and better economists, and this requires re-allocating our resources, financial and physical, in favour of university teaching. It would surely be good 'economy' if a sizeable share of the Ford Foundation grants (such as are now being distributed among the centres of economic research, most of which are unconnected with a University) are utilized, with due discrimination, for extension of the activities of our University Economics Departments by way of library facilities, tutorial instructions, etc., and, on top of all this, for the award of special fellowships enabling deserving scholars to go abroad for advanced training in recognized centres of economic studies. In so far as Ford Foundation funds are in dollar, this latter would not present any foreign exchange problem. In a country where economic studies, in spite of age in calendar years, are yet in their infancy, you cannot afford to restrict your consumption only to home-made Economics.

# 22

# A CENTRE FOR THEORETICAL ECONOMICS*

## I

Indian economists, particularly of the older generation, have been somewhat allergic to theory. It is about half a century that Economics has been functioning as a separate subject in our universities—the Economics Department of the University of Calcutta had its Golden Jubilee the other day, and the other older universities may perhaps follow suit soon. Economic Theory has also been a compulsory subject in the postgraduate course in all the universities in the country. And yet till recently very little work of any importance has been done in this field. Interesting factual and historical studies have been done in our universities, not unoften with a little mixture of politics and policy formulations. But economic theory as such, which is supposed to give direction to factual studies and to form the basis of policy prescriptions, has remained altogether a neglected branch of study in the country. Isolated cases can no doubt be cited of individual workers attempting to fill in small gaps here or there in the structure of economic theory. But substantial contribution to the advancement of the science—which is what theoretical research should aim at—there has been hardly any.

This is surprising. The Indian mind is traditionally speculative and is supposed to lend itself more to abstraction than to crude reality. Are not our ancestors builders of philosophical systems which provide sustenance to thinking minds even today? And have not our scholars made notable contributions to other sciences even in the modern age? Considering the general intellectual tradition of the country one would surely expect Theory rather than Organization to have been more congenial to the Indian economist. And yet this is just what has not happened. If one looks at the history of economic studies in India, one is impressed by a certain lack of direction and system in them; useful as they are in their own way as 'description' of the Indian economy, there is little attempt in them at generalization. It is remarkable how indifferent we have been to economic theory all these years.

Why this? It would be wrong to say that there was no provocation.

* Presidential Address to the *43rd Annual Conference of the Indian Economic Association*, Sec. IV. Originally published in *The Indian Economic Journal*, Vol. VIII, No. 3, January, 1961.

Stagnation itself ought to have been enough provocation to the economic theorist. The properties of the so-called subsistence economy, trade nexus between the agricultural sector and the urban sector, the character of primitive accumulation—all these provided substantial piles on which to build a structure of economic theory. Ingredients of such a theory had indeed been already there in Smith and Marx. Yet little attempt was made to put them together and to evolve a theory in adaptation to our economy. Nor was any creative interest shown in the contemporary marginalist theory. We shunned the so-called 'western economics', but the endeavour to replace it was lacking.

## II

Lamenting the failure in America, despite Carey's brilliant intuition, to produce a theory of economic progress alternative to classical political economy, Schumpeter has said: 'Well, opportunity is only a necessary and not a sufficient condition for a great performance. It does not itself produce the man capable of using it. And the brains that could have done the job were producing boots.'[1] Now the charge that our brains also were producing boots would surely be gratuitous. Yet the fact remains that Economics did not attract the man capable of building a theoretical system. The pioneers of Indian economic thinking, great as they were in many respects, were not economic theorists. In their impatience with the liberal tenets of classical political economy which were obviously at variance with the requirements of our economy, they repudiated even the tools of analysis that it provided. This was damaging to the progress of economic theory in the country. For even when economics came to be adopted as a subject for academic study, the influence of the early pioneers persisted, and there grew a distrust concerning Theory as such. The fact that contemporary economic thought was dominated by the marginalist theory of value which was far too remote from the needs of our economy added to this distrust.

These old inhibitions are disappearing. The post-war development of economic theory is too close to our problems not to have evoked response from our economists. And some of them, mostly of the post-war generation, have made notable contributions to it in recent years.

## III

Economics is not one of those branches of study which can have any complaint these days on the ground of public apathy. Rather the

[1] J. A. Schumpeter, *History of Economic Analysis* (London, 1954), p. 518.

contrary. Here as elsewhere the public are perhaps placing more weight upon our science than it ever was designed to bear. Economics is no longer treated as just an instrument of interpretation, as previously it used to be; it is today treated also as an instrument of operation. And large sums of money are being spent on research in this field. In our own country, apart from the normal expenditure on economic studies in universities, a sum of about 20 million rupees has been specially devoted to economic and social research during the last seven years, Ford Foundation alone having contributed about 10 million rupees for the purpose. The return that we are getting in the form of empirical studies is also not inconsiderable. If this process continues for some time, we may reach a stage when our economists will cease to have any complaint regarding data.

While, however, empirical research is being given the encouragement that it rightly deserves, not enough is being done for theoretical research. It will perhaps be argued that creative theoretical work depends on individual initiative and is better done at the universities as part of their normal activity—that it is empirical research that needs organization and team work and has to be undertaken by special agencies. There is force in the argument. And if our universities were properly staffed, perhaps one could leave things there. As it is, however, one would ask for more. Taste for theoretical work in the field of economics, as in other fields, too, is a matter of individual temperament. Even today not many among the economists of our country are interested in the technique of analysis, and not all of those who are interested are in the country. Could we not get some finance for a centre which might attract these men and where they could pursue a systematic and sustained study of analytical economics, untrammelled by pressures arising out of immediate problems? I think that it should be possible and that we need it.

*Note*—Since the above was written, the University Grants Commission has recognized a few Universities in the country as advanced centres for Economics, for which special grants are provided.

# 23

# ECONOMISTS AND THE GOVERNMENT*

## I

Speaking in 1934 before a London School of Economics audience (of which the present writer happened to be one), Professor Pigou gave a piece of warning to students of economics which deserves special notice today in our country. It is possible, he said, for a student of economics to construct arguments for whatever policy he would want to support. He may thus have the temptation to make slight adjustments in his economic view in favour of the policies and methods of one politicial party or the other, for that way lies his chance of playing a part in the great affairs of the State. A political party, be it the Government or the Opposition, does not have patience with a truth-seeker. It needs advocates, and in its scale, that economist weighs more who can find arguments in support of the policy to which it is wedded.

Professor Pigou cites an incident from his own experience. On a piece of economic legislation in his country he happened once to write a note in *The Times*. The Prime Minister of the day, thinking that it lent support to his policy, made a public acknowledgement of it in which he hailed its author as 'the great Cambridge economist'. In truth, however, the note did not favour the Government policy, and like a true scientist the Professor pointed this out. Whereupon in the estimation of the eminent Prime Minister, he came down as a 'mere academic theorist'. It is not always easy to put up with such vicissitudes of career; the temptation to seek public recognition is great. But for the social scientist to yield to such temptation is, Professor Pigou warns, 'to sell his birthright in the household of truth for a mess of political pottage.'[1]

As it is, economics in India centres on planning, and in this area there is quite a large scope for the economist to push 'opinion'. Gone are the days when an economist could find comfort in his cloistered abode manipulating curves and symbols and showing 'tendencies' under assumed conditions. Academic aloofness is at a discount in the economists' market these days. The economist must come out in the open, must act, if he is to be anybody in society. Up to a point this is good. In an economy which is in a state of transition,

* Originally published in *The Economic Weekly*, Special Number, July, 1962.

[1] A. C. Pigou, *Economics in Practice* (London, 1935); p. 10.

where big changes are taking place in every field of activity, there must occur stresses and strains which the economist cannot afford to overlook. We have seen a lot of these during the operation of the Second Plan, and we are up against some again as the Third Plan is proceeding. In the circumstances involvement in immediate problems is unavoidable for the economist. Planning does seem to indicate a revival of Political Economy.

## II

The trouble with us is not that we do political economy. The trouble is that political economy has often a tendency to degenerate into crude propaganda. Professor Pigou's warning is directed against this latter. Political Economy, let us remember, is the art of shaking out, under prescribed norms, the implications of theory for policy. And in so far as policy is embedded in theory, it has been in the best tradition of economic thinking to lay it bare. Professor Pigou's own practice upholds this tradition; economic science, he insists, must be 'fruit-bearing', and not merely 'light-bearing'. 'Let it be granted to the economist that, in his science as in others, from a diligent pursuit truth will not fly. But, if the final justification of his work is the fruit of practice, benefit through knowledge to human welfare, to *find* truth is not enough. Somehow the truth must be carried from the study to the market-place. Somehow it must be brought to the mind and utilized in the work of those persons who guide affairs.'[1]

But it is one thing for the economist to use his special knowledge in a disinterested way, for guiding public policy, it is an entirely different thing for him to twist economic propositions in favour of this or that political party. In a society such as ours which is obsessed by politics, where to be a politician is the surest way to public applause, surer even than to be a film star, and where the worth even of a scientist is measured by the number of committees that he serves and the frequency with which his name appears in newspapers, the danger that your economist should succumb to the temptation of using whatever abilities he may have for political ends is great indeed.

The danger is enhanced by the fact that, on the one hand there is yet insufficient awareness of the responsibilities of a citizen in the country, on the other hand we do not have anything like a leadership among economists. In an environment like this it is often easier for an economist to prosper as a critic of the Government than as its supporter. If you are a known supporter of Government policy, you have more chance of being on Committees; if you systematically oppose Government policy, you are made a hero. It is one of the

[1] Ibid., pp. 24–5.

tragic paradoxes of our democracy that our vocal public are, if anything, anti-Government. Nothing delights our audience in an assembly more than when the speaker runs down a Minister or the Government in general, even though the same audience might have been responsible for the ruling party being voted to power. Over the years we were taught to 'fight' a foreign Government; perhaps the inertia still remains, and the leaders who gave us the schooling now stand to bear the brunt.

Thus today, even as used to be the case before independence, a person catches public imagination more by writing a note of dissent than by signing an agreed document, however well-drafted the document might be. And if on top of this he can carry the foreign Press over to his side, his position as an economist is assured. Without him no Seminar is complete, no Association respectable. Even universities run after him offering distinction. For has he not shown a 'courage of conviction' and an 'independence of spirit' such as so many others have not shown? Amusing, yes! For one surely wonders in the present political set-up of the country what it is that one has to show courage against or to be independent of. The Government, as we have it now—and there is no reason why this tradition should not continue—does not punish opponents, it cajoles them, if only to preserve the reputation of being democratic. On the other hand, contrary to common belief, the economist today has better financial prospect outside the Government than within it. The critic does not suffer even if he is not 'bought up' by the Government.

## III

The atmosphere, if the picture drawn of it is true, is inimical to the growth of scientific attitude among economists. And yet it would be ungenerous to believe that there are not those among us who would be anxious to preserve the sanctity of our science, to go forward in their search for truth regardless of personal gain. Where will such men derive strength from? In the present race for 'the limelight and the applause', what is their position to be and to whom will they turn for sustenance and comfort? They will not go out of their way to please Ministers, nor will they seek popular approval. 'Evil is with them,' they will say to themselves, following Alfred Marshall, 'when all men speak well of them.' Must, then, they be left to themselves—each weaving his own net? One wishes they were. But there again the fear is that there will be a tendency to the building up of independent 'schools' of economic thinking. With one's experience of the fantastic novelties that some of our academicians are propagating in the university centres in the name of 'theory' (one gets a glimpse of these novelties mostly in examination answer-books), one does feel that the fear is a real one.

In the intellectually mature societies the problem is solved, even if in a rough and ready way, by the scientists themselves. In his Presidential Address to the American Economic Association Professor Paul Samuelson refers to the 'Happy Few' whose applause an individual economist seeks, expecting that the ideas which get churned within that charmed circle would find their way willy-nilly to those that directly guide policy. Some day somehow we shall have that here, too. Some kind of a leadership is bound to evolve among economists, as economic studies proceed along rigorous lines. Much of course will depend upon the behaviour of the younger generation who have yet to taste publicity. In the meantime, however, the Government may perhaps help the process. Even as it is, picking and choosing the right kind of economists should not be too difficult; given the will, the operation of Gresham's Law can surely be avoided in a controlled economy. A cautious method of selection would surely yield results. Having done that the Government may get a group formed round the Planning Commission for working out problems and for suggesting lines of investigation. The members of the group are not to be bound to any routine work. On the contrary they must be allowed to get on in their own way, keeping their allegiance to their respective universities. And yet it should be more than what the Panel of Economists have come to be. It should be a closer group than the Panel as it is constituted today, and unlike the Panel it should be associated with the Economic Adviser's Directorate rather than with the Ministers or Members of the Planning Commission who, after all, are not economists.

# 24

# WHY LAMENT FOR ECONOMICS?*

## I

In spite of Professor D. P. Mukherji's 'Lament for Economics',[1] economics is prospering. And it is prospering, not as a handmaid to sociology but in its own right. Economists have no doubt been social thinkers and some of them have made important contributions to social philosophy in a broad sense. But their contributions have been enriched by the fact that they had economic tools in their possession which they could use for the sharpening of their understanding of social phenomena. And these tools were devised with reference to a particular type of relationship between man and man—the type of relationship, that is, that finds expression in the market for goods and factors.

Professor Mukherji complains that Indian economists are Keynesians and wants them to be Marxians, if not 'Marxologists'. I happen to be an Indian and, if anything, an economist. I must confess that I am neither a Keynesian nor a Marxian. I am an eclectic. And I suppose most of the Indian economists are that. The Indian economist, I suppose, will agree to take the basic question that Keynes asks as the starting point of his enquiry. Living in an economy which has for years been stagnant and where unemployment is chronic, he cannot just escape the question why resources remain less than fully employed. He will perhaps agree also to take a few tools from Keynes's tool-box. But the answer that he will get and the 'social philosophy' that he will be led on to will be anything but Keynesian. In spite of the support that Indian economists have often given to the policy of deficit-financing in the context of economic planning, let it be understood very clearly that they are aware that they live in a non-Keynesian world where, on the economic plane, it is 'shortage of capital' and not 'deficiency of effective demand' that is responsible for stagnation and unemployment and where, to use Harrod's apt expressions, the 'warranted rate of growth' is *below* and not above the 'natural rate of growth'. To secure full employment we must invest more, but the process must be accompanied by an *increase* in the 'propensity to save'. This certainly is not Keynesian. At this point the Indian economists will perhaps turn to Marx or further back to Adam Smith. He may

* Originally published in *The Economic Weekly*, December 5, 1959.

[1] D. P. Mukherji, 'Lament for Economics', *The Economic Weekly*, November 14, 1959.

utilize the Marxian concept of 'economic surplus' or the Smithian concept of 'productive labour' to know what in his economic environment limits the possibilities of growth. This does not, however, compel him to go all the way with either Marx or Smith; the Indian economist, if anything, is an idealist and also a believer in interventionism.

Does Schumpeter help us? Schumpeter for whom Professor Mukherji shows such great enthusiasm? I suppose, not. Our society is not entrepreneur-orientated. If it were, we would have seen our growth level bumping against the wall of the 'natural rate' (*à la* Harrod) and making for chronic inflation. Our experience till recently has been just the other way round. The inflationary pressures that we have had in recent years are exogenous.

## II

No, we—Indian economists—have to be eclectic. We must borrow tools freely from many sources, even though the final structure that we build up may be our own. Can we, however, shun other disciplines in this pursuit? Professor Mukherji says, No. For he believes that the science of society—which is 'human science'—is an indivisible whole. 'It is one social science distinguishable from natural science. It is not a "synthetic" product, nor is it merely an interrelated corpus of sciences.' I have always found it difficult to understand this—shall I say—biological interpretation of sciences. Well, if you stand for it, why not push it further and bring natural science, too, within your orbit? Science *is* search for truth; and truth (they say), like God, is indivisible. Why, then, differentiate human science from natural science?

I believe differentiation is an essential process in the building up of a corpus of knowledge, as it is in the building up of an organism. I believe in the Smithian doctrine of division of labour. Let economists, political scientists, psychologists and historians specialize in their respective fields. Let these disciplines be 'compartmentalized', and let the totality of knowledge grow. He who has vision can then effect the desired integration and try to discover, as Marx did with the then existing body of knowledge, the vital links that connect social movements.

One word of caution to our 'model-builders' for whom I am pleading. Let them not, in their intoxication with 'model-building', forget that if they are to be economic practitioners—as they may need to be—they must know the character of the social environment into which the models are proposed to be projected. Here is the occasion for the economist to take assistance from other disciplines. I would not expect the economist to cultivate these other disciplines himself; there are others to do that. But the economist, if he is to be of use to society, must not divorce himself from what is happening outside his own field. Do the more 'brilliant' among our younger Indian economists need this warning? I wonder.

# 25

# REFLECTIONS ON HIGHER EDUCATION IN INDIA IN THE LIGHT OF THE ROBBINS REPORT*

## I

The Robbins Report on Higher Education[1] has had an enormously enthusiastic reception in the United Kingdom. The Government has welcomed it and ministers have commended it as 'the most important social document to be produced since the Beveridge Report'.[2]

Undoubtedly the report will have far-reaching effect on the volume and pattern of university education in arts, sciences and technology in Great Britain if a good part of the 178 recommendations that it has offered is implemented, as of course it will be. The Committee, as Lord Robbins put it in a Press interview on the day of the publication of the report, was inspired by a sense of urgency created by the prospect of an educational crisis that the country must face—the demand for higher education running too far ahead of the supply of provision for it. It thus recommended the establishment of twenty-eight new universities, in addition to the thirty-two existing today, so as to accommodate altogether an estimated 560,000 students coming up for enrolment in universities in 1980–1, as compared with 260,000 today.

There has been for quite some time a sense of dissatisfaction at the slow pace of expansion of universities in this country. And indeed, judging by growing demands for trained personnel from defence, industry and teaching itself, the dissatisfaction was perhaps justified. Obviously the social forces released in the wake of the Second World War have been too progressive to permit continuance of what was perhaps too conservative an attitude; the appointment of the Robbins Committee is itself evidence of an awareness that rethinking on the subject was urgently called for.

And yet even here there have been voices expressing misgivings at

* Originally published in Minerva, Winter, 1964.

[1] *Higher Education. Report of the Committee appointed by the Prime Minister under the Chairmanship of Lord Robbins. 1961–63.* Cmnd. 2154 (London: H.M. Stationery Office, 1963).

[2] *Social Insurances and Allied Services.* Report by Sir William Beveridge, K.C.B. Cmnd. 6404 (London: H.M. Stationery Office, 1942).

the amount of expansion suggested in the report and the principle underlying the estimates. *The Times*, for example, was quick to point to the possible danger of setting 'demand for places' as the criterion of expansion of universities. 'The change of scale, the influx of students of questionable bent, the thinner spread of first rate teachers are bound to influence profoundly the nature and quality of British universities.'[1] The fear is genuine and how far the traditional standard of university education in Great Britain will succeed in surviving this big leap will be a matter for educationists all over the world to watch.

My purpose here is not to criticize the Robbins Report or to commend it as such; there are others to do that. I would rather be concerned with an assessment of the possible repercussion of the Robbins proposals for expansion in the field of higher education on the thinking of educationists in my own country. For I am pretty sure that an important document such as the Robbins Report will not go unnoticed in India where there are men eager to seize anything that happens in the so-called developed countries to show how backward we are in relation to these countries. We adopted the British system of education more than a century ago and we have got accustomed to it. Now we may very well be tempted to follow the British model of growth. For is not our *per capita* expenditure on higher education still too low as compared to other countries and is not the rush of students for admission in our universities too much for the existing institutions to bear?

## II

The state of university education in India does pose a problem and, judged by the increasing number of admission-seeking undergraduates and graduates, the problem appears to be similar to that which confronts the Robbins Committee. And yet paradoxically, the solution of the problem in India is not to accelerate the growth of universities but to decelerate it.

Already there is a tendency in India to judge the progress of higher education in terms of the number of universities set up and the number of students coming out with an MA or M.SC degree. In recent years, particularly since the establishment in the early fifties of the University Grants Commission,[2] the multiplication of universities has been too rapid. Some of us have viewed this tendency with considerable alarm. The first university in India of the modern type—the University of Calcutta—was established in 1857. At the

[1] Leader on the Robbins Report, *The Times*, October 24, 1963.

[2] The University Grants Commission became a statutory body by an Act of Parliament in 1956. But it started operation in December 1953 when it came into existence under an executive order of the Government of India.

turn of the century, the country had only five universities—all essentially of the affiliating type, with postgraduate teaching centralized in one or two. Even as late as 1919 when the Calcutta University Commission, presided over by Michael Sadler, submitted its report, the number had come to only seven, two more universities having been established during the First World War. The Sadler Commission which recommended, among other things, the establishment of small universities of a residential teaching type, gave a sudden spurt to the spread of universities in the country. Even then, between 1921 and 1929, only about ten universities were added, and at the time of independence in 1947, altogether there were just about twenty universities in the country with an average population of perhaps not more than 2000 in the residential universities. Considering the growth in the number of students genuinely desirous of pursuing higher education in arts, science and technology, the rate of growth of centres of higher education (twenty universities in the course of about a century) in the country could be judged as rather moderate. In this respect, as in others, we followed the British tradition rather than the American.

Then came independence in 1947 and the University Education Commission in 1949, presided over by Dr S. Radhakrishnan (now President of the Indian Republic) and in their wake a tremendous momentum in the growth of universities in the country. Whereas at the time of the Radhakrishnan Commission the number of universities in India was twenty-five, now within just about fourteen years, it has gone up to no less than fifty-five.[1] We have thus already achieved in this field a growth rate of about 9 per cent per year, whereas the Robbins Committee recommends for Great Britain an annual growth rate of just about 5 per cent.

## III

Now, in a country which has for years been politically dependent and where progress in every field of activity has been slow, it is not surprising that the attainment of freedom should have released forces making for an 'unbalanced growth' and that those fields of

[1] As many as thirty-five of these universities are teaching and affiliating; the rest (i.e. twenty) are strictly teaching and residential (or federal). In the former, a large share of the responsibility of teaching, particularly undergraduate teaching, is distributed among affiliated colleges. This enables these universities to expand indefinitely, the enrolment in some running to over 50,000. Besides the full-fledged universities, there are seven institutions such as the Indian Institute of Science, Bangalore, and the Indian School of International Studies, New Delhi, which are 'deemed as universities under Section 3 of the U.G.C. Act'. Further, there are eight institutions, such as the Indian Statistical Institute, Calcutta, which have been 'declared as institutions of national importance by Act of Parliament'. They are all treated as universities and have the right to confer degrees.

activity should have received undue stimulus where investment was comparatively less complicated and where the return on investment could not be readily estimated. The establishment of universities in particular is one such field of activity, and no wonder India has gone ahead with it since independence.

It appears, however, that expansion in this field has been a little too rapid, leading to a visible depression in the standard of teaching and research. It is because the Robbins Report may provide a further fillip to this tendency to 'overproduction' by providing the legitimacy of a British model that it appears to be so significant from the point of view of India. If indeed the need for universities is to be assessed by the number of places that our candidates coming out from secondary schools are likely to demand—and this is by and large the measuring stick of the Robbins Committee—then the expansionist programme of the University Grants Commission, as it is being operated in India, would surely be justified. The major universities in India are surely overcrowded (even some of the residential universities carry more than 10,000 students on their rolls) and, if the potential candidates for university education were all to be accommodated, surely there would be a need for more universities.[1] The matter, however, is not so straightforward.

In England, where a certain minimum standard of intellectual equipment can be assumed in prospective candidates for university education and a certain minimum of intellectual opportunities are guaranteed in university centres, *demand* for places may well be permitted to set the criterion of *provision* for places. Indeed the broad motivation of the Robbins Committee is, as they underline in their report, 'the undoubted gain to young people of being brought into contact with leaders of thought and of knowing themselves to be members of an institution in which the highest standards of intellectual excellence are honoured'.[2] This surely is a large claim and perhaps justified in terms of the standards exhibited in British universities, especially Oxford and Cambridge. But if the truth is to be told, not many of the universities in India, even as the number stands at present, can have pretensions to a standard such as is urged in the Robbins Report. The staff/student ratio in our universities, particularly in the arts faculties, is too low—in some cases as low as 2:100. The workload of teachers is too high, averaging in most universities fifteen hours a week and—what is worse—involving too many subjects for each teacher to teach. Library and laboratory facilities and, paradoxically, recreation facilities are poor. One could thus go on enumerating the deficiencies of our universities—no

[1] The total enrolment in universities in India in 1962–3 was 1,082,666 as compared to 980,046 in 1961–2—a 10 per cent increase in just one year.

[2] Robbins Report, op. cit., para. 464, p. 151.

wonder there are such frequent strikes in our university centres! It is towards the improvement in these spheres that our resources should be directed, and it is for its appreciation of standards in these spheres, if not for its general approach, that Indian university reformers might profitably turn to the recommendations of the Robbins Committee. We need a consolidation of the existing institutions more than an increase in numbers—a 'deepening' rather than a 'widening' of capital, to use the economist's terminology, in the field of higher education.

## IV

Finances are severely limited by the poverty of the country and so is the availability of suitable teachers for running centres of higher learning and research.[1] By Indian standards, the salary scales of university teachers are not too bad; the maximum in the professor's grade is Rs 1500 per month (=£1350 per annum) which is about sixty times the *per capita* income in the country. But judged by Western standards they are unattractive; the British salary scales are about two and a half times as high as those prevailing in India. It is thus not possible, within the limits of our finance, to supplement the local supply with imports of talents from abroad, even if we wished to do so. On the other hand, some of our own people are being attracted away to foreign countries. To add to this, there is a growing demand for trained personnel from government and industry, thanks to the planned economic development of the country. Those of us who have experience on selection committees in our universities know how terribly difficult it is to staff even the major universities in the country. There is little doubt that the multiplication of universities has resulted in a deterioration in the standard of our teaching staff, not to speak of the average standard of students enrolled for higher studies.

In the present state of higher education in India, one would indeed like to have our universities, barring the older ones which have over the years established a tradition of learning and research in many fields and where a sense of the right standard has taken root, curtail the range of their operations and specialize in a limited number of subjects, subsidiary fields of study being kept at the undergraduate level. The introduction of an inter-university 'division of labour' will both increase the efficiency of operation of each

[1] Cf. *Vice-Chancellors' Conference 1961*, University Grants Commission and Ministry of Education, Government of India (New Delhi: New Age Printing Press, 1962). *Vice-Chancellors' Conference 1962*, University Grants Commission and Ministry of Education, Government of India (New Delhi: New Age Printing Press, 1963). Summaries of both these documents have been published in *Minerva*: I (1963) 2, pp. 209–16 and 4, pp. 508–21.

university and prevent an unduly wide dispersal of whatever talents we have in a particular field. This latter consideration is a good deal more important than is generally recognized; there is such a thing as 'external economy' in the concentration of resources and it applies to intellectual pursuits as much as it does to production of material commodities. Higher studies and research flourish in an atmosphere congenial to intellectual intercourse and for this to be fruitful a university needs a certain minimum number of scholars interested in the same field.

There are indications that the principle of specialization suggested here has begun to receive some recognition in our country in recent years. Among the new universities there are a few which have been designed for work in specific fields, as, for instance, the Universities of Jadavpur and Kalyani in West Bengal, specializing in engineering and agriculture respectively. Not that humanities are not taught in these centres; but their status is recognized as subsidiary to the main field. Thus far, this approach is confined primarily to technology and agriculture. The University Grants Commission has, however, recently introduced a more general approach which recognizes the dangers of dispersion. It has designated a few major universities as 'advanced centres' in respect of particular branches of study, such as economics, mathematics, physics, etc. While all universities will do these studies up to the postgraduate and research levels, the so-called advanced centres will be given special grants for expansion in the appropriate fields. The move is in the right direction. This does indeed accord with our principle of specialization and one can expect that the advanced centres being few in number, as far as any particular field of study is concerned, and being specially favoured by the University Grants Commission, will be in a position to secure adequate staff and other facilities so as to be able to attain and preserve a reasonably high standard of intellectual excellence.

However, one must not forget that it is not enough to have a collection of talents on the teaching staff; the centres must also be assured a steady flow of students who could do justice to the staff and facilities provided. If the chosen centres attract not merely superior teachers but also the better type of students, all will be well. Since, however, the choice of these centres will inevitably be based on suitability for particular fields of study as judged in terms of their cultural and environmental setting, there is a chance that many deserving students will find them too far away to be able to attend. If this happens, the training resources of the centre will be under-employed and Indian society will fail to get maximum returns from the scheme. One remedy against a possible maladjustment of this kind is to introduce a generous system of scholarships to enable qualified and deserving students to attend the favoured centres. This indeed is an inevitable supplement to the discriminatory allocation of funds that the scheme involves. But grants of stipends or scholarships may not always overcome the inertia of our students and their parents; geographical distance may prove to be too much of a barrier in a country of India's size. It may be necessary, therefore, for the University Grants Commission to see that the centres are as widely dispersed over the country as possible and that the need for special financial incentives to attract good students is minimized.

One possible way of tackling the problem is to divide the country into five or six zones and to have each zone provided with, say, one advanced centre for each of the major fields of study. These centres may be suitably distributed among the universities located in each zone, so that although any particular university may be asked to specialize in just one or two fields and some perhaps in none at all, the zone as a whole is provided with enough centres to meet legitimate local demands. Another, not necessarily alternative, way is to create, under the auspices of the University Grants Commission, a special category of professors on an all-India basis, preferably on a higher scale of salary than is prescribed for ordinary university professors. The posts might be made transferable and the professors distributed among the universities in which there is a steady flow of good students but which are inadequately staffed. There is also a case for holding at regular intervals refresher courses under the auspices of the advanced centres which university teachers from various parts of the country might attend and from which they might derive guidance and enlightenment. A beginning has already been made in this direction in one or two centres with financial support from the University Grants Commission. The process needs to be extended and regularized.

## V

The University Grants Commission has a great task before it, for the future of our country will depend very much upon the lead it gives to the country's higher education. Unfortunately, as it is constituted at the moment, it cannot possibly bear the responsibility that rests on it. Barring the Chairman, the members of the commission are all honorary, having as vice-chancellors full-time tasks in their respective universities. The staff of the secretariat is also not adequate.[1] Besides the Secretary, there are just about half a dozen officers on whom rests the main burden of assessing the requirements of the various universities with all their complications. They are thus over-

[1] The secretariat of the U.G.C. consists, besides the Secretary, of one Joint Secretary and one Deputy Secretary, altogether with fifteen senior and junior officers. There is no research staff attached to the Commission.

worked, each having to deal with nine to ten universities on the average. The Robbins Committee recommends one full-time chairman, two full-time deputy chairmen and twenty part-time members for the University Grants Commission, which it proposes in place of the existing University Grants Committee. Here perhaps India may be advised rather to go somewhat *beyond* the Robbins Report. If only because of the country's heterogeneous character, higher education, as indeed education in general, is vastly more complicated in India than in Great Britain and it requires more direction and control. Although the states have a responsibility in this sphere, quite a large part of finance for higher education is supplied by the central government, and the University Grants Commission is the agency through which the central finance is distributed. It is surely up to the Commission to watch how the finance is utilized. The area of its operation has expanded enormously since the University Grants Commission was instituted in the early fifties and yet we have practically the same constitution governing it. It is time that the government put the Commission on a firm basis, with at least half a dozen full-time members, besides the full-time Chairman who is already there. There is need for a larger secretariat too, with research officers attached to it. It is poor economy not to spend a little more on a body on which so much of our future depends.

## VI

The general approach to higher education in India suggested here would naturally imply a reduction in the proportion of school-leaving boys and girls going to university. Does this mean that those who fail to enter the university should be left without further education or training? This is by no means the inevitable conclusion. Far from it. The planning of education does not mean only the setting up of universities or higher technical institutes. There are various other fields of training which can fill the gap between the higher secondary stage and the university. In the context of India one would like to see a very much greater extension of polytechnics for training in management, accountancy and secretarial work and also engineering and technological schools of various types for turning out skilled operatives—centres, that is, of vocational training, whose place in the economy should be of the highest importance.

Nor does our plea for restricting entry into universities mean that deserving candidates should be denied places. What is emphasized here is diversification of opportunities. A good many of our boys and girls apply for university places simply because they have no alternatives available to them. If the pressure on our universities is to be reduced, these boys and girls have to be given outlets suited to their abilities.

Further, while there is an overall deficiency of teaching staff in our universities, there is excess capacity in certain institutions employing persons capable of university teaching. There is no reason, for example, why our national laboratories and other research institutions should confine themselves to research alone; they might be asked to co-operate with universities which are located near them and to undertake a share of postgraduate teaching. A link between the two will benefit both; while teaching will be enriched by active research experience, it will in its turn act as a stimulus to research. Since our research institutions relate mostly to science and technology, this co-operation will also help a certain re-allocation of places within our existing universities, favouring expansion of these fields as against pure arts—a re-allocation which is called for in view of the present state of the economy of the country.

There is an educational crisis in India. But, unlike the crisis in Great Britain as diagnosed by the Robbins Committee, the crisis in India arises from defective quality rather than from insufficient quantity, and it is towards the improvement of the quality of our universities that the efforts of our educationists should be directed. With reference to the Indian universities, 'more means worse' is perhaps not such an inappropriate slogan after all.[1]

[1] Cf. Lord Robbins' speech in the House of Lords, *The Times*, December 12, 1963.

# INDEX

Made in the USA
Las Vegas, NV
19 September 2026

4c77578c-50bf-42c6-8bc3-bab221de477dR02